ISLAM:
A Dictionary

Ruqaiyyah Waris Maqsood

Stanley  s) Ltd

Dedicated to my dear friend and brother, M. Aslam Arain.

The author and publisher give grateful thanks to E. H. Bladon for her generous comments and meticulous eye for detail.

Illustrations by Kathy Baxendale, Celia Hart

Maps on pages 82–4 by Barking Dog Art

First published in 1996 by:
Stanley Thornes (Publishers) Ltd
Ellenborough House
Wellington Street
CHELTENHAM GL50 1YW
England

96 97 98 99 00 / 10 9 8 7 6 5 4 3 2 1

A catalogue record for this book is available from the British Library.

ISBN 0 7487 2560 1

Typeset by Tech-Set, Gateshead
Printed and bound in Great Britain by Redwood Books, Trowbridge, Wiltshire

GUIDE TO USING THE DICTIONARY

Introduction

This short dictionary is designed to help you understand the key terms, and to know something about the key people, places, events and practices you will need for the Islam component of the GCSE examination.

Signposts

None of these terms can be taken in isolation; we understand things best when we see them in context. To help you do this, certain words appear in bold type. These words are signposts directing you to look elsewhere in the dictionary. For example, if you look up **jamarat**, you will find a description of three stone pillars in Saudi Arabia. But you will understand their significance much better if you look up the other words highlighted there, because then you will be able to place jamarat in the context of the hajj and other religious events and symbols.

Five words – Allah, Islam, Muslim, Prophet and Qur'an – appear so frequently throughout the book that they have not been highlighted; otherwise they might take your attention away from less obvious signposts.

Pronunciation

Many of the words in this dictionary are in Arabic, the language of the Muslim scripture and of Muslim prayer. Try to learn the correct pronunciation of these terms. Remember that Arabic has some sounds and letters that do not exist in English. Some Arabic speakers make a clear distinction with these sounds, while others find them impossible to pronounce and use sounds which are as close as they can get. For example, many Muslims of the Indian subcontinent cannot pronounce the Arabic 'dh' but say 'z' instead (thus we have mu'adhin or muezzin).

Unfortunately, text books differ in the way they represent Arabic words in English. For example, the name of the city to which all Muslims turn in prayer might be Mecca in one book and Makkah in another. This is because Arabic has a different alphabet and when we write Arabic words in English letters we can usually only give an approximation. That is why, in some cases, this dictionary gives more than one version of the same word, and basically follows the spellings suggested on the recommended list for GCSE.

The pronunciation guide (set out in *italics*) is simple to follow. Two sounds worth noting are: (1) *aa* (see *aa-kee-kaa* for Aqiqah) – this indicates a long 'a', as in '*baa baa* black sheep'; (2) a single consonant (see the *d* in *ab-d* for Abd) – this should not be spoken as though you were naming the letter in the alphabet, but as though you were demonstrating how to pronounce it.

Sometimes the endings of words in Arabic change when they are followed by words that begin with a vowel. For example, words that end in 'ah' become 'at' when followed by a vowel – salah (prayer) becomes salat-ul-asr and zakah becomes zakat-ul-fitr.

Some letters (*d, l, n, r, s, t, z, sh, th, tha, tza*) alter the pronunciation of 'al' (the) at the start of a word. For example, al-salah is pronounced 'as-salah', and al-rahman becomes 'ar-rahman'.

References
Throughout the dictionary, you will find number references in brackets. Unless otherwise stated, these refer to the Qur'an. The number before the colon gives the chapter, or surah, in the Qur'an; the number(s) after the colon refer to the particular verses, or ayahs, within that surah.

A

Abd (*ab-d*) Arabic for 'servant' or 'slave'. The word commonly forms part of a Muslim name, the other part consisting of one of the names of God (e.g. Abdullah meaning 'servant of Allah', and Abd al-Karim, 'servant of the Generous One' – *al* is Arabic for 'the'). The Muslim name Abdul is, of course, a shortened version of the full name. (7:180; 17:110; 20:8; 59:24).

Abd al-Muttalib (*ab-d al-mut-ta-lib*) the Prophet's grandfather, a chief of the **Quraish** clan Hashim, and a famous **hanif**. The Prophet was only six when his mother died and Abd al-Muttalib cared for him until he himself died two years later.

Abdullah (*ab-dul-laah*) the Prophet's father, a merchant, who travelled to many distant cities. He married his cousin, **Aminah**, but shortly after she became pregnant he was taken ill and died. Thus he never saw his son who was to become the Prophet of Islam.

Abortion removal of a foetus (baby in the early stages of development) from its mother's womb to terminate pregnancy. Islam allows **birth control** to prevent pregnancy, and some scholars allow abortion for valid reasons up to the 16th week, when it was assumed that the child's **soul** had entered its body. However, modern X-ray and ultra-sound equipment now shows the full development of the unborn child as a separate living entity from conception. All Muslims reject the deliberate termination of a life. The only exception may be if the life of the mother is in real danger, when some scholars allow abortion on the grounds that her existing life takes precedence over that of her unborn child. Others disagree and grant both equal rights. (17:31).

Abraham ▶ see **Ibrahim**.

Abu Bakr (*a-bu bak-er*) d.634. He was the Prophet's closest friend, a merchant and the first adult male **convert** to Islam. His daughter **Aishah** was the Prophet's third wife. He was a gentle, generous, quiet man, easily moved to tears of compassion, and was elected the first **caliph** of Islam after the Prophet died (ruled 632–4). He was known as As-Siddiq ('witness to the truth') and Amirul Muminim ('ruler of the believers'), the first of the 'rightly guided caliphs' or Rashidun.

Abu Talib (*a-boo taa-lib*) an uncle of the Prophet, and the father of **Ali**. After the Prophet's parents and grandfather died, Abu Talib took him into his care. He never became a Muslim, but he protected the Prophet courageously throughout his life. The Prophet loved him dearly, and always regretted that he rejected Islam.

Adam (*a-dam*) the first prophet. He and his partner Hawwah (Eve) were the first human beings on earth, created to be the representatives of Allah. They were equal, being created from a single **soul** (4:1). The **angels** were concerned that beings with **free will** would cause chaos, and **Shaytan** the chief **jinn** refused to honour Adam (15:28–31). His pride and disobedience were the origin of **evil**. Adam and Hawwah originally lived in innocence and happiness, a state described as 'a garden' (not to be confused with **Paradise**). They had been forbidden to eat the fruit of one tree. Shaytan deceived them into disobedience by suggesting it was the 'tree of eternal life' (20:120), and tempted them to try to live on earth for ever. By eating the fruit, the humans showed a lack of faith in **life after death**, and lost their innocence; in hoping to be free of dependence upon Allah, they also lost the real meaning and purpose to life itself (2:35–9; 7:19–27; 20:120–22). When they realised this loss, it brought **tawbah**; they turned back to Allah and were reunited and forgiven at **Mount Arafat** – the event remembered in the **wuquf** during the **hajj**. In Islam there is no inherited original sin or need for a saviour; every individual human faces

Judgement Day for their own decisions and actions. ▶ See also **amal, forgiveness, Isa**.

Adhan (*a-than*) the public call to **prayer**, made loudly so that Muslims know it is time to leave what they are doing and go to the mosque to pray. You will find the words of the adhan on page 81. ▶ See also **Bilal, iqamah, mu'adhin**.

Calling the adhan from a minaret.

Adultery ▶ see **zinah** (24:6–10).

AH this is the abbreviation for Anno **Hijrah**, 'the year of the migration', the year in which the Prophet left his home town of **Makkah**, which had consistently rejected his call to Islam, and moved to **Madinah**, a town to which he had been invited as ruler.

Muslims take all following dates from this year, the first year of the success of Islam.

Ahl al-Bait (*aal al-bay-t*) the 'People of the House', the immediate family and dependants of the Prophet. ▶ See also **Prophet's family**.

Ahl al-Kitab (*aal al-kit-ab*) ▶ see **People of the Book**.

Aishah (*a-yee-shah*) the daughter of **Abu Bakr**. She was the Prophet's third wife. Some traditions suggest that she married the Prophet when she was only six years old. She was either 18 or 28 when the Prophet died. Famous for her quick wit and good memory, she was one of the chief sources of information about the Prophet and is known to have corrected many wrongly reported **hadith**. She was once falsely suspected of **zinah**, and a Qur'anic **revelation** was given especially to show her innocence (24:11–19). The Prophet died in her arms and was buried in her room. She continued to teach and be involved in Muslim politics until she died at the age of over 70 in 58 AH, respected as a great scholar and recorder of hadith.

Akhirah (*ak-hee-rah*) the hereafter, **life after death**. Descriptions of conditions in **Paradise** and **Hell** are given in detail in the Qur'an, but most scholars believe these are to be interpreted metaphorically, since the Qur'an states that 'We will not be prevented from changing your forms and creating you again in forms *you know not*' (56:60–61). ('In **Heaven** I prepare for the righteous believers what no eye has ever seen, no ear has ever heard, and what the deepest mind could never imagine' – **Hadith qudsi**). A person's life after death will depend very much on three things: what they have believed, how they have lived, and the mercy of Allah (82:19). A person's deeds during their lifetime are recorded in their own 'book' by two recording **angels**, and will provide evidence on **Judgement Day**.

Akhlaq (*ak-laak*) a person's character, as shown in their conduct, attitude and ethics.

Akhwan al-Muslimun (*ak-wan al-mus-lim-oon*) ▶ see **Muslim Brotherhood**.

Al-Amin (*al-aa-meen*) the 'trustworthy one', a title given to the Prophet when he was a young man by the people of **Makkah**, in recognition of his outstanding honesty and upright character.

Al-Aqsa (*al-ak-saa*) the **mosque** with the silver dome in the old walled city of **Jerusalem**. It was built in 715 by **Caliph** Walid at the place where, according to tradition, the Prophet commenced his ascent through the heavens on the Night of Ascent (▶ see **Laylat-ul-Miraj**, 17:1). This was on the site of the old palace and royal stables of King **Suleiman**.

Alcohol forbidden in Islam as khamr (*kam-r*) – a substance that intoxicates or poisons the mind. Alcohol was drunk by the tribesmen of the Prophet's time, causing similar social problems to those it brings with it today. However, the ban on alcohol took a long time to develop. First there was the warning that both good and **evil** come from the same substance (16:67 and 2:219); then the request that people should not come to **prayer** with alcohol in their body (4:43) – which effectively banned alcohol, since Muslims pray five times a day – and finally there was the order not to drink it at all (5:93–4). In some Muslim societies (e.g. Saudi Arabia), the law lays down harsh penalties even for possession of alcohol.

Al-Ghaib (*al-ray-b*) the unknown – aspects of reality which are beyond human perception. Muslims admit that the part of God's **creation** known about by humans is only a tiny fraction of the whole; most of it (whole universes, orders of created beings and so forth) lies beyond human awareness or imagination. Included in al-Ghaib are such things as the exact nature of **angels** and **jinn**, and matters such as knowledge of the time of our **death** and our state of being in **Akhirah**. (6:59; 7:187; 16:77).

Al-Ghazzali (*al-ra-zaa-lee*) a famous Muslim scholar (1058–1111), professor of Islamic theology in Baghdad and Sufi mystic. At first persecuted by the Muslim **ulama**, he eventually convinced them of the soundness of his theology and was one of the leading scholars who protected extreme **Sunni** orthodoxy from losing sight of mystical devotion. ▶ See also **Sufism**.

Al-hamdu-li-Llah (*al-ham-doo-lil-laah*) 'all thanks be to Allah', an expression used frequently to show gratitude and awareness of Allah's blessings. It also expresses modesty, as a Muslim would say this in response to some compliment. ▶ See **hamd**.

Ali (*aa-lee*) the prophet's cousin (son of **Abu Talib**) and husband of the Prophet's daughter **Fatimah**, he ruled as **caliph** (656–61). He was known as the Lion of God (Asadullah), and showed his courage when he was converted to Islam at the age of ten, and declared his willingness to defend and serve the Prophet even if all others turned against him. As the Prophet's lieutenant in battle, and father of the Prophet's grandchildren, many felt he should have been the first caliph after the Prophet's death, but he accepted the leadership of the 'elders' **Abu Bakr**, **Umar** and **Uthman** before he took his turn 24 years later. He fought in the battle of the Camel against **Aishah** in 656, and the battle of Siffin against **Mu'awiyah**. His followers formed the **Shl'ah** (now called **Shi'ites**), and continued to favour the leadership of the **Prophet's family** line. He was murdered whilst at **prayer** in the **mosque** at Kufa. He had foreseen the event and had asked that the assassin be shown mercy.

Al-Kafi (*al-kaa-fee*) the title of the books of **hadith** compiled by Muhammad Ibn Yaqub Koleini, a **Shi'ah** scholar.

Al-Khulafa-ur-Rashidun (*al-ku-laa-faa-ur-raa-shee-doon*) the 'rightly guided **caliphs**', the first four successors to the prophet. ▶ See **Abu Bakr**, **Ali**, **Umar**, **Uthman**.

Al-Kiswah (*al-kis-waah*) the Arabic name for the black cloth draped over the shrine of **Ka'bah**, and lifted during the **hajj** to show the building beneath. It is made afresh each year, because traditionally at the end of hajj it is cut up and distributed to the pilgrims as souvenirs. Special pieces are sent as gifts to various **mosques** and celebrities. Verses from the Qur'an are embroidered in gold thread round its edges.

The Ka'bah shrine, covered with the black cloth.

Allah (*al-laah*) the Muslim term for God, the Almighty One, the Compassionate, the Merciful, the source from which all things seen and unseen have their origin and return. In the **revelation**, Allah has many names, all revealing qualities and attributes. You will find them all listed on pages 79 to 80. One term never used is Abb or 'Father' – so common in the Jewish and **Christian** traditions – presumably to prevent Muslims from thinking of God in human, paternal terms.

Allahu Akbar (*al-laa-hoo ak-baa*) the cry 'Allah is the most great', used in Muslim **prayers** and as an expression of loyalty towards God or encouragement to Muslims in many circumstances. ▶ See **adhan**.

Almohads properly known as al-Muwahiddun (*al-mu-wa-hid-doon*) from *wahid* meaning 'one' (literally, those who believe in the oneness of God). This North African Muslim dynasty, active from 1121 to 1296, was in rivalry to the **Almoravids**. They were founded by Muhammad Ibn Tumart of Sus. By 1163 they had entered Andalusia, and ruled most of Spain and all of North Africa. The last great Almohad was Ya'qub (1184–99). Almohad rule in Andalusia gradually disintegrated but lingered in Africa until 1269, when they were replaced by the Hafsids in Tunisia and the Moravids in Morocco.

Almoravids properly known as al-Murabitun (*al-mu-ra-bit-oon*) from the concept of *ribat*, or religious fortress. This dynasty in North Africa was **converted** in the third century

AH by the **marabout** Ibn Yasin, and was led originally by Yusuf bin Tashifin, who founded Marrakesh in 1062. They subdued all Morocco and central **Maghreb**, ruling from 1076 to 1147, and drove back the advancing **Christians** in Spain. They deposed the Andalusian Amirs and became the masters of Muslim Spain from 1090 to 1145 CE. ▶ See also **Almohads**.

Al-Qadr (*al-kaad-er*) the key Muslim doctrine of Allah's complete and final control over events, or destiny. This is one of the most difficult of all theological concepts – how can the idea of God knowing absolutely everything be balanced with the idea that a human being has **free will**? If God knows in advance everything that will happen to a person, then that person's life must be entirely predestined. This leads to such cases as that of a thief pleading innocence, because he was predestined to steal. However, fatalism is an abuse of Islam, and not true practice. Muslims are expected to listen to God's **revelations** to humanity through the mediation of chosen **prophets**, and to make choices and adjust their lives accordingly (6:91; 23:23). The concept of judgement in Islam depends on personal responsibility, even if God always knows from the outset what the ultimate fate of each individual **soul** will be. If a person chooses *this* then the consequences will be *that*. However, we must remember that we often need the experience of mistakes and misfortunes to learn lessons, and Allah the Merciful allows for all circumstances. Muslims learn to trust Allah. ▶ See also **Judgement Day, tawakkul.**

Amal (*am-aal*) this is the concept of action. To be a Muslim one must have **iman** (faith) and amal (action). Faith is worthless unless it translates into a good way of life; actions are worthless without faith. In other words, the expression of pious belief is meaningless from a hypocrite who does not put those beliefs into practice.

Aminah (*aa-mee-nah*) the mother of the Prophet. She had a short and sad life, marrying her cousin **Abdullah** and being widowed whilst pregnant with her only child. The infant Prophet was given to the custody of a Bedouin wet-nurse (Halimah), and brought back to Aminah when he was weaned. Aminah died when the Prophet was only six years old.

Angels in Arabic, malaikah (*mal-ay-ee-kaa*). These are part of **al-Ghaib**, beings created by Allah 'of light', as humans are created 'of earth'. They have no **free will** but always act to bring about God's will. Their functions include bringing messages and warnings, and acting as 'protecting friends' (41:30–32); also, particular angels are assigned to each individual to keep the record of their deeds (82:10–12). Among the named angels are **Jibril**, the messenger frequently spoken of in the Qur'an as the Holy Spirit, Israfil (the caller of **souls** on **Judgement Day**), Azrail (the angel that takes souls at **death**), Munkar and Nadir (the questioners of souls), Mikail (protector of holy places and life-sustainer in times of trouble), Malik (the keeper of **Hell**), the Ridwan (the keeper of **Paradise**).

Anger anger was disapproved of by the Prophet, who always advised against hasty action. If people felt angry when standing, they should sit down; or if sitting, they should lie down. However, Islam has always justified an active response against cruelty, **tyranny** and oppression.

Animals these should always be treated with respect and consideration in Islam. Fox-hunting, badger-baiting, cock- or dog-fighting and such like 'sport' are totally forbidden. So is the exploitation of animals for luxury use, although Muslims are encouraged not to waste animal products that result from the normal death of the animal. ▶ See also **hunting, slaughter**.

Ansar (*an-saar*) these were the 'helpers' or 'supporters' of **Madinah** who were kind to the Muslims who had made the **Hijrah** from **Makkah** leaving all their possessions behind: they took them into their own homes and cared for them.

Aqiqah (*aa-kee-kaah*) some Muslims cut the hair of a baby seven days after birth, and donate its weight in silver or gold in **sadaqah**. Parents of bald babies usually offer a gift too. Some parents also offer the meat of an animal or two (or part of one, depending on what they can afford)

as the basis for a feast and to distribute to the needy. Others give the equivalent in cash. None of these practices is compulsory ▶ See also **birth ceremonies**.

Arabesque a decorative flourish in writing or **art**.

Arafat, Mt ▶ see **Mount Arafat**.

Arranged marriages most Muslim societies do not approve of free mixing between the sexes after puberty. It is then the parents' duty to arrange the best possible marriage for their children. They inquire carefully into the character and background of any intended partner. In some societies marriage is encouraged as soon as the youngsters are tempted to become sexually active, and this can mean brides as young as ten years old. This is illegal in the UK. The Prophet insisted that prospective spouses should at least see each other, and both freely agree to the marriage. Marriage is not regarded as 'made in **Heaven**', but as a contract. If it fails, the couple are free to **divorce**, and then remarry.

Art all pictorial representation of Allah, **angels**, the Prophet or previous **prophets** is forbidden in Islam. So are any kinds of statues that could lead to idolatry; for, according to the ancient law Allah revealed to **Musa**, humans should not make graven images and bow down to them. Some scholars take the view that *all* statues should therefore be forbidden; others see no harm in ornaments or toys such as dolls that do not suggest **idol** worship. Statues of kings and politicians are particularly disapproved of (although very common in some Muslim countries). The Prophet had all art-work removed from the places where he prayed. The more extreme scholars forbid the painting of humans or animals, but allow scenic views, plants and trees; an alternative point of view allows all art on fabric such as paper, cloth or wood, so long as it is two-dimensional and does not encourage lust, pornography or nationalism. **Photography**, pictures on TV or video, classroom teaching materials, and incomplete statues are all permitted provided they follow the same rulings.

Ascetic ► see **zahid**, **zuhd**.

Ashurah (*ash-oo-rah*) the 10th **Muharram**, the commemoration of **Musa** leading his people to freedom from the Pharaoh. The Prophet always fasted on this day, and many **Sunni** Muslims follow this practice. **Shi'ite** Muslims, for whom devotion to the **Prophet's family** is a crucial element, celebrate Ashurah as the anniversary of the death of his grandson **Hussein** at **Karbala**. They hold processions, passion plays, and occasionally practise blood-letting with knives and flogging themselves with chains. Sunnis do not regard Hussein's death as any more special than that of any other martyr.

Asr or salat-ul-asr (*saa-lat-ul-as-er*) – the compulsory **salah** made at any time from mid-afternoon until a short while before sunset.

Awrah (*ow-raah*) literally, 'ornaments'. It refers to that which a man or woman may not show to others out of modesty (► see **clothing – rules of modesty**). Scholars vary in their interpretation of it. A few think it means literally the personal **wealth** and jewellery which should not be shown off, but generally it is used to mean 'private parts', and it is **sunnah** for Muslim women to cover everything except their faces and hands from those outside their family. ◄

Ayah (*ay-yaah*) literally, 'a sign' – a verse of the Qur'an.

Ayatollah (*ay-a-toll-aah*) meaning literally 'sign of God', this is the title given to the leading **Shi'ite imam**. The most famous ayatollah of modern times was the Iranian Ayatollah Khomeini, the leader of the people's revolution against the Shah of Iran in 1978–9.

Ayyub (*ay-yoob*) a **prophet** who lived in the Petra region of Jordan, famous for his **sabr**. He was a wealthy tribal sheikh who was struck down with misfortunes by **Shaytan**, but who never faltered in his faith in Allah. (6:84; 21:83–4; 38:41–2).

B

Backbiting ► see **slander**.

Badr (*bad-er*) the site of the Prophet's first famous battle, in 624 CE. The Prophet and a small force of Muslim soldiers took on a much larger army sent from **Makkah**, and successfully defeated them. (3:13).

Baitullah, Bait al-Haram (*bay-tul-laah*, *bay-tal-ha-raam*) Arabic names for the **Ka'bah**, the 'house of God' in **Makkah**.

Bait ul-Maqdis (*bayt ul-mak-dees*) the **mosque** with the golden dome in **Jerusalem**, on the site of the altar of the temple built by the **Jews** for the one true God. It had been destroyed by the Romans, and Jews were forbidden to go there. When **Caliph Umar** took control of Jerusalem, he started the clearing of the site with his own bare hands, and the temple area became the third most holy place of Islam. The word **Maqdis** comes from *qds* meaning 'holy'; the mosque is also called al-Quds, and the Dome of the Rock.

Barakah (*ba-raa-kaa*) a sense of blessedness, peace and joy – an awareness of the blessings of Allah. Frequently this refers to a powerful

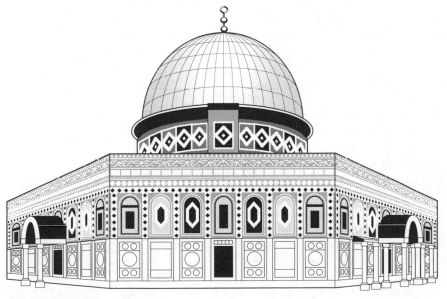

The Dome of the Rock, Jerusalem.

atmosphere felt at certain shrines and sanctuaries, places where people pray or feel moved by beauty and awe, or presence of **angels**.

Barzakh (*baar-zak*) the barrier between this world and the next – the place or state in which people will be after **death** and before **Judgement Day** (23:99–100). ▶ See also **al-Ghaib**.

Begging asking for money without working for it. The Prophet taught his companions that it was better to earn money by any honest means, no matter how lowly, than to beg from others.

Bidah (*bee-daah*) an innovation or practice that has been added to Islam without the authority of the Qur'an or **sunnah**. **Ulama** should be able to justify their teaching easily from these two sources, and any person being required to do something not specified in these sources has the right to challenge it. Bidah does not refer to practices of everyday life; for example, it is not bidah to use a knife and fork, modern toilet, modern technological equipment and so forth. It *is* bidah to try to insist that things that the Prophet left to personal choice are a compulsory part of the faith of Islam – for example, performing extra **prayers**, growing a beard, wearing a turban.

Bilal (*bee-lal*) an Abyssinian slave, one of the first Muslims. He was tortured by his master Ummayah, who staked him out in the sun with a large rock on his chest, but **Abu Bakr** purchased his freedom. He had a very fine voice, and became the first **mu'adhin**. ▶ See **adhan**.

Birth ceremonies Muslim babies are welcomed into the family of Islam by having the **adhan** whispered into their ears shortly after birth. The tahnik is the folk ceremony of touching the baby's lips with something sweet, symbolising the hope that they will develop a sweet nature. **Aqiqah** usually takes place after about a week, when the mother has recovered. It is **sunnah** to feast on the meat of sheep or goat. Money may be offered to charity (▶ see **sadaqah**), and sweets to friends. The baby should be given a Muslim **name**, which must not be boastful of qualities the child may not grow up to have. ▶ See also **Bismillah, khitan**.

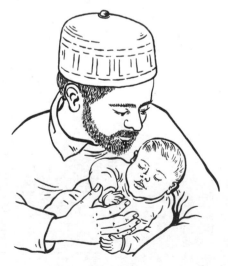

Whispering the adhan.

Birth control family planning is not forbidden to Muslims, so long as the form of control is one that is agreed openly by both parents, and is not done secretly or forced by one partner. It must be a method that prevents conception (for example, the condom, the Pill, or withdrawal), and not a form of **abortion** after conception.

Bismillah (*bis-mill-aah*) literally, 'in the name of Allah'. This word also refers to a family party given when a child (or adult **convert**) has learnt the Arabic alphabet and can recite by heart a few **surahs** of the Qur'an.

Ornamental calligraphy reading 'Bismillah ir-Rahman ir-Rahim'.

Bismillah ir-Rahman ir-Rahim (*bis-mill-aah ir-raah-man ir-raa-heem*) literally, 'in the name of

Allah, the Compassionate, the Merciful', the phrase with which Muslims begin any action or endeavour, whether it be eating a meal or setting out on a journey. It is also the preface to every **surah** of the Qur'an except the ninth.

Black Stone in Arabic, al-Hajr al-aswad (*al-ha-jer al-as-wad*). This is a stone set in one corner of the **Ka'bah**. Traditionally, it is supposed to come from **Heaven** and to have originally been white; this may well refer to its meteoric origin – it was 'white' or star-like as it fell through the atmosphere, and a black lump when it was found. Originally set in the shrine by **Ibrahim**, it was washed out by a flash-flood at the time of the Prophet. The tribal leaders argued over who should have the honour of replacing it, and eventually agreed that God should decide – it would

The Black Stone.

be the next man who passed by. This was **al-Amin**, who solved the problem by inviting representatives of all tribes to lift it on his cloak.
▶ See also **hajj**, **tawaf**.

Blood sports ▶ see **hunting**.

Buraq (*bu-rak*) the name given in Islamic tradition to the creature which transported the Prophet in a flash to **Jerusalem** on the **Laylat-ul-Miraj**.

Burial Muslims should be buried in simple **graves**, usually just with a marker, perhaps bearing the name and dates of the deceased. Bodies are considered to be nothing but decaying remains of that which was used by the **soul** while living on earth; they return to the soil, while the soul goes to **Akhirah**. Expensive coffins and gravestones are therefore just a waste of resources. Before burial, the body is treated with respect, washed carefully, and shrouded in white cloths (two for a man, five for a woman). A special **prayer** (the **salat-ul-janaza**) is recited, and the deceased is taken to a burial ground to be laid to rest, one person to a grave, on the right side with the face turned towards **Makkah**. It is considered more respectful at a funeral to walk in procession rather than ride in a car, and to carry the body on a reusable stretcher. Muslims are encouraged

not to **mourn** ostentatiously, but to have confidence in life after death and faith in Allah's mercy on the soul of the deceased.

Burqa (*bur-kaa*) a word of Persian origin, used by Urdu speakers to refer to the all-covering garment worn by some Muslim women in various societies. The 'shuttlecock burqa', so called because of its shape, can be seen in Afghanistan and northern Pakistan. It has a little grid through which the woman sees. These coverings are not specified in Islam, and the amount of covering worn by a woman cannot indicate the quality of her faith. ▶ See also **hijab**.

An Afghan burqa.

C

Calendar the Muslim calendar is a lunar one; consequently the feast days are 11 days earlier each solar year. Year 1 is taken to be 622, the year of the **Hijrah** when the Prophet migrated from **Makkah** to **Madinah**. To calculate a Muslim year, take 622 from the year in the calendar, and multiply it by $\frac{33}{32}$.

Caliph in Arabic, khalifah (*kaa-lee-faa*) – a successor to the Prophet, someone who rules, or bears responsibility, on his behalf and, beyond him, on behalf of Allah. The first four caliphs were the Prophet's companions **Abu Bakr** (632–4), **Umar** (634–44), **Uthman** (644–56) and **Ali** (656–61). These four were known as **al-Khulafa-ur-Rashidun**. Following them, the caliphate went to **Mu'awiyah**, the first of the **Ummayyad** caliphs. His successors were challenged by Ali's descendants. The Ummayyad family won the day, but many of the caliphs of this line were corrupt and betrayed pure Islamic principles. Other famous family lines of caliphs include the Abbasids, the **Fatimids, Safavids, Mughals, Almohads, Almoravids**, and **Ottomans**.

Calligraphy the art of beautiful writing with particular reference to texts of the Qur'an. Since pictorial art is discouraged in Islam, great emphasis is placed on ornamental calligraphy. Writers of the Qur'anic texts were expected to be extremely pious and devout people themselves.

Ornamental calligraphy on a tile.

Capital punishment putting an offender to death, a common penalty for many offences before the coming of Islam. In the Qur'an it is limited to cases of murder (2:178) and active treason. In Islam, after trial and sentence, the fate of the murderer lies in the hands of the victim's family; they are entitled to choose equal and just revenge, or to take

diyyah. The Prophet commented that the very best response was **forgiveness** even for murder, and to leave punishment to Allah. (5:67; 17:33). ▶ See also **qisas**.

Celibacy choosing to live without a sexual relationship. **Christian** monks, nuns and hermits have regarded celibacy as a form of piety and purity. However, in Islam **sex** is regarded as one of God's compassionate gifts to humanity, and therefore to reject it is a form of ingratitude, even a dangerous practice which may result in character and emotional problems. ▶ See also **kafir**.

Chador (*cha-door*) a sheet-like garment used by Muslim women in some societies (e.g. Iran) to completely cover themselves. It is not necessarily of black fabric – this is a matter of tradition and not of Islam. ▶ See also **burqa**, **hijab**.

Cheating being dishonest in order to gain advantage. This is forbidden in Islam. If a Muslim cannot be honest he or she has really left Islam. (5:9).

Children the Prophet forbade any cruelty to children, and also disapproved of spoiling them. They should be cared for, and trained to lead good lives. It is the responsibility of their parents to see to their education as far as possible, have them trained in a trade or means of earning a living, and arrange their marriages wisely.

Christians the followers of the Prophet **Isa** (Jesus), the Christ or Mashih (Messiah). True Christians are commended by the Qur'an for their charitable, noble and compassionate lives (5:85–8), and their devotion to God (2:62). However, Muslims believe that Jesus never claimed to be the son of God, except in the sense that we are all God's children. Therefore they reject the Trinitarian Atonement-Saviour doctrines, which they compare to the Baal-worship opposed by all the **prophets** of the Old Testament, or the 'mystery-cults' (such as Mithraism) common in the Roman Empire. These doctrines are condemned as **shirk**, added later to Isa's pure message. Christians are urged to respond to the call of Islam. (4:171; 5:75, 80).

Circumcision ▶ see **khitan**.

Cleanliness in Arabic, taharah (*taa-ha-raa*). Muslims regard personal cleanliness as of prime importance. Bodies and clothing should always be as clean as possible (▶ see **ghusl**, **instanja**, **wudu**). The Prophet particularly recommended special cleanliness of hands, mouth, hair and private parts.

Clothing – rules of modesty both male and female Muslims are required to dress modestly. Men should always be clean and smart, and covered at least from navel to knee. Women usually cover everything except their hands and face. It is regarded as immodest to wear clothes that are tight, transparent, or cling to the female shape, making the woman 'naked although clothed'. Clothing is not in any set style, although certain societies have very strong traditions. It is not correct Islam for any woman to be forced to wear a particular garment, and it is an abuse of Islam to oppress women for showing their faces. Muslim men, when confronted by improperly dressed women, are required to look away, not to approach, rebuke or harass them. (24:30). ▶ See also **burqa**, **chador**, **hijab**.

Consciousness of God ▶ see **taqwa**.

Conversion by the sword this is something Muslims are often accused of by the West, without much factual evidence. The Qur'an recommends **tolerance**: 'Let there be no compulsion in matters of faith' (2:256). The code of practice for Muslims when conquering a territory was to offer people the chance of converting to Islam or of declaring allegiance to the new government and paying a tax instead of doing military service. ▶ See **Dhimmi**.

Converts Muslims claim that Islam is the religion of natural reason and that therefore all children are born Muslims; only as they grow up are they influenced to accept whatever is the religion of their parents. People who convert to Islam as adults often say they are 'coming home', because of the feeling known as **din-ul-fitrah** or reversion, rather than conversion.

Corporal punishment this includes any physical punishment, such as flogging. Muslims condemn cruelty, but they believe in such punishment for a person who apparently cannot be persuaded by any other means to behave in a socially acceptable way. Corporal punishment is therefore not forbidden in schools, and is carried out in some Muslim societies for social offences such as drunkenness, sexual lewdness in public, and **theft**. ▶ See also **hudud**.

Creation according to Islam, God alone is the creator of our universe (▶ see **al-Ghaib**) and Allah is totally different in kind from any part of creation. Muslim scholars keep an open mind towards all scientific theories, on the grounds that what is regarded as true today may be disproved tomorrow. ▶ See also **First Cause**.

Crusades the term refers to the eight major attempts between 1095 and 1291 of various armies (under the banner of Christianity) to recapture **Jerusalem** from the Muslims who had ruled there since **Caliph Umar**'s occupation in 638. Jerusalem changed hands several times, but the city was Muslim when the British partitioned it in 1948.

D

Dajjal (*daj-jaal*) the Anti-Christ – in Muslim tradition, an evil creature who will rule the earth for 40 days before **Judgement Day**. It will be defeated by the return of **Isa**, who will destroy it before the **end of the world**.

Darud (*da-rood*) a blessing on the Prophet **Muhammad**; a prayer often recited at the end of **salah**.

Dar-ul-Islam (*daar-ul-is-laam*) the 'house' or 'dwelling place' of Islam. It has two main meanings: the hearts of true believers; and places where Islam is practised.

Da'wah (*daa-waah*) an invitation, call, or preaching. The term applies more broadly to the duty of Muslims to invite others to find the **Shari'ah** – the 'straight path' of Islam. The call should always be carried out with wisdom, gentleness, tact and good manners. Aggressive and arrogant preaching cannot qualify as da'wah, since it drives people *away* from Islam.

Dawud (*daa-wood*) the Arabic name of the shepherd-prophet David, the slayer of Jalut (Goliath) and successor of Talut (Saul) as king of the tribes of Israel from c.1000 BCE. He captured **Jerusalem** and made it his capital after ruling from Hebron. His **revelations** from Allah are known as the **Zabur**. His most famous son was the **prophet Suleiman**. (2:247–51; 6:84; 21:78–80; 34:10–11; 38:17–26).

Day of Resurrection ▶ see **resurrection**.

Death Muslims believe that death is simply the state of a body as its soul passes from one form of life to the next, which, **insha Allah**, will be better for us. Life on earth is one of God's gifts, and our **souls** will be recalled when God pleases. We should not fear death – Allah knows the time of our deaths from our conception in the womb, or even before – we should simply live every day we have on earth in the best possible way we can. (3:145, 185; 4:78). ▶ See also **burial**.

Death of the Prophet the Prophet became ill with fever and violent headaches at the age of 63. When he realised he was dying, he asked to be moved to the room of his beloved **Aishah**, and for **Abu Bakr** to lead the prayer in his place. He died with his head in Aishah's lap, and she recorded his last words as: 'Nay, but I have chosen the most exalted companions, in **Paradise**.' He was buried in Aishah's room in **Madinah**.

Dervish from darwish (*dar-weesh*), the 'sill of the door'. A dervish is a Sufi who practises particular methods and **dhikrs** to gain a special feeling of closeness to God. The most famous 'orders' are the 'whirling' dervishes (who practise sacred dance), and 'wandering' dervishes (who do not live in a fixed home). ▶ See also **Sufism**.

Destiny ▶ see **al-Qadr**.

Devil ▶ see **Shaytan**.

Dhikr (*thik-er*) from *dharaka*, to remember, think, relate. The deliberate concentration on Allah while doing such things as chanting certain phrases or repeating the 'beautiful names'. You will find these listed on pages 79 to 80.

Dhimmi (*thim-mee*) non-Muslim citizens living in Islamic states, where they are expected to pay taxes for the services, care and protection they should receive.

Dhul-Hijjah (*thul-hij-jaah*) the last month of the Islamic **calendar** year, in which the **hajj** takes place.

Din (*deen*) from *dana*, to owe or be indebted to, this is usually translated as 'religion'. Din means much more than just a set of beliefs; it means being consciously aware of personal love and gratitude towards God, and the decision to live in a manner befitting this relationship.

Din-ul-fitrah (*deen-ul-fit-raah*) the belief that 'truth stands clear from error' (2:256), and that Islam is the belief based on reason, and the natural way of life for all pious thinking persons. ▶ See **converts**.

Dishonesty being untruthful in word or action. A person who has departed from the truth has departed from Islam – you can fool other people, but you can never fool God.

Divination the practice of trying to discover in advance what will happen in the future, in order to benefit from the knowledge; or the belief that various fetishes and objects have the power to alter **fate** or fortune. This leads to the idea that such objects have more power than God; according to the Qur'an, it is therefore a form of **shirk**, and such things as crystal balls, tarot cards, astrological practices, spiritualism, and so on, are forbidden in Islam. ▶ See also **istikhara**, **magic**, **trust**.

Divorce the breaking up of marriage. Of all the things allowed by God and the Prophet, this is the one which carries most disapproval. It is allowed when one or both partners deliberately refuse to fulfil some part of the marriage contract. This may involve physical or mental cruelty, desertion, unacceptable behaviour (e.g. drunkenness, violence, criminal activity), refusal to satisfy the partner physically, or deliberately turning away from the faith. Whatever the problem is, every effort should be made to help put it right, but if all else fails, a partner has the right to divorce and be free of the one who has departed so far from Islam. Once divorce becomes inevitable, it should be carried out humanely and fairly, without unpleasant pressures or recriminations, and great attention should be paid to the care of any children involved. The father has legal custody, but the children normally live with their mother, unless circumstances are much more favourable with the father. (2:228–41); 65:1–7; 4:35, 128). ▶ See also **khul, lian, talaq.**

Diyyah (*di-yaah*) this is the financial compensation (or blood money) for injuries or **death**. The relatives of a victim of murder or manslaughter can choose to accept diyyah rather than have the killer condemned to death. The more mercy the injured parties show, the more they are praised and blessed by Allah. ▶ See **capital punishment.**

Dogs Muslims do not keep dogs in the house, because a dog's tendency to show its natural affection and to salivate freely would make it very difficult for the owners to stay in **wudu**. However, dogs are often kept as companions outside the house, and work for example as guard dogs or sheep dogs.

Dome of the Rock ▶ see **Bait ul-Maqdis.**

Dowry in Arabic, mahar (*maa-her*). This is the payment of an agreed sum of money to the intended wife. It is often paid (at least partly) in advance, and should be completed at the wedding. This money belongs exclusively to the bride, and is hers to keep should her husband later **divorce** her. The larger the mahar, the less likely he is to divorce; but seeking a large mahar is not in keeping with the principles of Islam. Neither is making it a present to the bride's father or family leader, or not agreeing to pay it at all. The question of dowry should never be used as a reason to insult a woman, or keep her 'prisoner', or force her to remain unmarried (2:229, 236–7; 4:4, 19–21, 25). The bride's family should certainly not pay a dowry to the husband or his family – practices abolished by the Prophet.

Drugs in Arabic, khamr (*kam-r*) 'intoxicating substances'. Medicine is allowed in Islam, although preferably the drug should not contain any **alcohol**. Drugs used for 'pleasure', or 'getting high', such as hashish, marijuana, cocaine, heroin, 'smack', and 'crack', are blamed for many of today's social problems, and are totally forbidden (5:93). If any quantity affects one's judgement, one should not take even the tiniest amount.

Du'a (*doo-aa*) private prayers, personal requests that are not part of the **salah**. Although a good Muslim should accept with patience whatever God sends, it is considered only natural to ask for help, understanding and **forgiveness**. The Prophet did this constantly. However, instead of wasting time begging God to let you pass an exam, or not let your sick relative die, it is better to work hard and pray for the insight to know what is the right thing to do, or for the ability to keep calm in order to be of most use. ▶ See also **sabr**.

Dunya (*doon-yaa*) the word means 'the world', but in Islam it refers specifically to the attractive and tempting things of this world that draw people away from right living. The world itself cannot be **evil**, because it is the creation of Allah; but clearly there is a great deal of evil around in it, which has to be encountered, resisted, avoided or, ideally, removed. 'Worldly' things include money, possessions, ambition, jobs/careers, leisure pursuits, and so on. (2:212; 3:14).

Making du'a prayers.

E

Empowerment of women the Qur'an is clear on the matter of all believing men and women being entirely equal in worth, spirituality, responsibility, and so on (33:35). The religious and moral duties of male and female Muslims are exactly the same. These ideas have never been accepted readily by societies where men control power in government, at work, and in the home through their wages, and this is still true of some Muslim cultures, just as it is of other male-dominated societies. However, the Qur'an demands equality and fairness for women in education and other opportunities, and in property laws and **divorce** settlements.

End of the world According to Islam, the existence of the earth, solar system, universe and cosmos is entirely dependent upon the will of its creator, God. It may seem eternal, but it could collapse in the twinkling of an eye. The only element which is eternal is God, who alone knows the time the world will end. ▶ See also **al-Ghaib**, **dajjal**, **Judgement Day**.

Envy Muslims should not be envious of the fortunes of others for Allah grants our circumstances as tests (4:32). Our **wealth**, success, health, good fortune – these may suddenly change. The Prophet recommended that people who are tempted to envy others should 'look down, not up', meaning they should be grateful for what they have and consider the lives of those less fortunate than themselves.

Equal rights for women ▶ see **empowerment of women**. One aspect of fairness for women is to take into consideration their physical wellbeing and to be genuinely considerate to women who are menstruating or involved in childbirth or childrearing. Muslim men are expected to protect and maintain women (4:34) without denying their rights. When the Qur'an says that women have equal rights 'but men are a degree above them' (2:228) this is often taken out of context – it refers to divorce-law. The word 'but' is better translated as 'for'; it reminds a man leaving his wife and children that he has an obligation from Allah to continue to take care of them, since he is usually in the better financial position.

Euthanasia the practice of deliberately causing **death** for merciful reasons, usually to relieve suffering. It might involve 'putting to sleep' by injection, or quickly finishing off in some other way a badly wounded person who would otherwise die slowly. In Islam the practice is illegal. Efforts should always be made to heal and relieve pain. No one has the right to end another person's life. No one but Allah knows when a **soul** is ready to depart the body; the time of suffering before death may be the time when a soul finally understands its relationship to Allah. Moreover, suffering in this life may help to make up for sins committed, and for this reason it would be wrong to rob someone of this opportunity.

Evil the deliberate desire to act in a way contrary to the will of God. The inevitable cost in a world where God has allowed **free will**. ▶ See **Shaytan**.

Evolution the theory that human beings are descended from animals, probably apes. Islam regards all animal life as having been created by Allah, but keeps an open mind as to the process. Some Muslims accept the theory of evolution, others feel it is still far from having being proved.

Extended families families which include such relatives as grandparents, uncles and aunts, and perhaps more than one wife.

Extremism going to extremes implies fanaticism, **tyranny** and the desire to compete, none of which are Islamic qualities. The fact that some people are naturally more pious or enthusiastic about religious practices than others does not necessarily mean they are more virtuous. Out of misplaced enthusiasm, extremists often try to impose unnecessary religious burdens on others. (5:90; 31:19). ▶ See **zealotry**.

F

Fajr or salat-ul-fajr (*saa-lat-ul-faj-er*) – the first compulsory **salah** of the day, between first light of dawn and sunrise.

Fanaticism ▶ see **extremism**.

Fard (*far-d*) compulsory. Certain aspects of Islam are regarded as compulsory, and others are considered voluntary (or **nawafil**) matters. The **five pillars of Islam** are all fard, for example. In most matters, however, general principles are fard but the details of working them out are voluntary. For example, it is fard to be modest, but you are left to interpret for yourself how to dress or behave modestly, provided you respect Islamic laws.

Fard kifaya (*far-d kif-ay-aa*) the duty of Muslims to organise, provide or employ the necessary services and facilities needed for the welfare of any community; for example, doctors, teachers, suppliers of water, clothing, food, housing, electricity. It also refers to duties such as making the **salat-ul-janaza** if the deceased has no relative to do it.

Fasting in Arabic, sawm (*saw-m*). This is the practice of subjecting the human body to discipline for the sake of spiritual benefit (2:183–4). The purity and self-control involved are more important than the going without food. Many Muslims fast frequently, but the only compulsory fast (▶ see **five pillars of Islam)** is that of the month of **Ramadan**, either 29 or 30 days, according to the sighting of the moon. During this month, no food or drink must pass the lips from first light of dawn to sunset, a length of time that varies according to the country one is in and the season of the year. One must also refrain from smoking cigarettes and cigars, and avoid all sexual activity during the same times. All these things are permitted during the hours of darkness (2:187). Anyone who might be at risk is excused from fasting; this includes children, those who are sick or need medical treatment, old people who are frail or ill, and women who are menstruating, pregnant, have just given birth or are breastfeeding (2:185), or are making an arduous journey. All these are encouraged to make up the days of fasting they have missed if this becomes possible before the next Ramadan.

Fate ▶ see **al-Qadr**.

Fatihah (*fat-ee-haah*) literally, 'the opener'. The opening **surah** of the Qur'an; used in every compulsory **prayer**, and therefore recited at least 17 times per day. You will find it written out on page 81.

Fatimah (*fat-ee-maah*) the fourth daughter of the Prophet, and the only one of his children to survive him. She married **Ali** and they had four children: two sons, Hassan and **Hussein**, and two daughters, Zainab and Umm Kulthum. She was very like her father in looks and temperament, and much loved. For her sake, the Prophet requested Ali not to take a second wife while she lived, which would have hurt her. She died shortly after the Prophet, aged about 29.

Fatimids (*fat-ee-mids*) a dynasty of Muslim rulers in Egypt, claiming descent from the Prophet through **Fatimah**.

Fatwa (*fat-waa*) pl. fatawa; the legal guidance of a pious and knowledgeable scholar on any matter of Islamic law, based on Qur'an, **sunnah** and Islamic **Shari'ah**.

Feasts celebrations in thanksgiving for such things as childbirth, personal triumphs and successes, marriage, and so forth. ▶ See **Id** entries.

Fiqh (*fik-h*) literally, 'understanding'. The study of Islamic law and jurisprudence. Experts in Islamic law are known as Fuqahah.

First Cause the origin of existence. Nothing exists at all unless it has been caused. A thing which does exist but might not have done is called 'contingent'. Everything that exists falls into this category – the sun, for example, might never have existed. The fact that it does exist means that it must have been *caused* by something. To say the universe was caused by the Big Bang does not answer the questions, what was it that 'banged', where did it come from, why did it 'bang', and so on. All causes either go on to infinity, which defies the logic of our minds, or there was a First Cause at some time, which lies beyond human understanding. Religious people, including Muslims, generally recognise this First Cause to be God. (3:47).

Five pillars of Islam these are the five compulsory duties required of a Muslim – **shahadah, salah, sawm, zakah** and **hajj.**

Food laws Muslim food should be **halal**, which means that it is allowed by God. All fruit, vegetable matter and seafood is in this category. Halal meat is from an animal that has been humanely slaughtered with a sharp instrument and the recital of a **prayer**. Muslims may not eat any product from the pig, or meat from an animal that has been sacrificed to **idols**, died of natural causes, been strangled or gored to death, or has not had the blood drained from it. Most Muslims examine carefully all the ingredients listed on packeted food to make sure it does not contain animal fats or gelatine – the animal fat could be non-halal beef or pork lard. Others will eat beef or lamb slaughtered in the UK as this is regarded as the meat of **Christians** or **Jews**, the **People of the Book**. However, no Muslim would eat any pork product. (2:172–3; 5:4; 6:145).

Forgiveness one of the key attributes of Allah. In every **surah** except one, Allah is revealed as the Compassionate, the Merciful. No matter what a person has done, if he or she is genuinely sorry, and truly wishes to be forgiven by God, then God will certainly forgive, 'even if' – as the Prophet said – 'your sins are as great as the earth itself'. What matters is genuine **repentance**, and a

real effort not to repeat the offence or mistake. God is not fooled by false repentance; and God's justice cannot be bought off with gestures like **sacrifices**. (22:37).

Free will the fundamental ingredient of human activity, and the most difficult of God's gifts to understand or appreciate (▶ see **al-Qadr**). Free will makes sense of human morality; without it, there is no such thing as good or **evil** conduct or action, for we would simply be automatons. In Islam, the whole of our future **life after death** is based on the decisions we make with our free will, and how we respond to conscience, faith and so on.

Friendship Muslims should be firm and trustworthy friends. However, they are advised to choose their companions carefully, for it is all too human to be influenced by the people closest to you, and some friends might lead you into bad ways. (3:28).

Fundamentalism in Islam this should imply simply being a believer who wishes to get back to the fundamentals of the faith, and who accepts the truths of the Qur'an and authentic **hadith**, and cutting through all the obscure scholarship that puts religion beyond the reach of simple folk.

G

Gabriel ▶ see **Jibril**.

Gambling trying to make money out of a game of chance. Some things contain both harm and benefit. If their harm outweighs their benefit, they are **haram**, or forbidden in Islam. Gambling may seem harmless fun at first, but it is like a drug, leading the gambler into wasting more and more money which should have been used for other purposes (2:219; 5:93). Therefore, such addictive pursuits as casino gambling, card games for money, fruit machines, Bingo and the National Lottery are all haram.

Generosity willingness to give – one of the key qualities in Islam (76:7–10). Muslims should always give, expecting nothing in return except that Allah will be pleased with them (2:264).

Ghusl (*roo-sul*) a full bath or shower to make one ritually clean. Necessary after sexual intercourse, menstruation, childbirth, or contact with a dead body. (5:7).

Gospel ▶ see **Injil**.

Graves places of **burial**. These should be very simple in Islam, and not luxurious monuments trying to impress or claim glory for the deceased. On the other hand, they should be obvious, so that people do not walk on them. The Prophet recommended a small raised mound with a simple marker at the head.

Simple graves.

Greed wanting too much of anything. Islam disapproves of greed in any form. One should be moderate in all things – moderate both in appetite and in one's desire to possess.

Green Islam humans are expected to be Allah's deputies in looking after the earth. They must not spoil or abuse their environment, but keep it healthy and productive and pleasant. Any spoiling activity such as pollution, destruction of trees, or unnatural and unpleasant methods of production (e.g. factory farming) is **haram** in Islam. (6:165; 45:12–13). ▶ See also **khilafah**.

Greetings the usual Muslim greeting is 'As-salaam alaykum' (*as-sal-aam al-ay-kum*), meaning 'Peace be with you'. The reply is 'Wa-alaykum as-salaam' (*wa-al-ay-kum as-sal-aam*) 'And to you also be peace'.

Guardian angels according to the Qur'an, everyone is allotted two special **angels** to be with them throughout life. They are called our 'protecting friends' (41:30–32). Their purpose is not so much to guard as to keep a record of a person's deeds, for **Judgement Day**. It is a positive record as far as possible – if someone is sorry for having done wrong, the bad record is wiped out. When people feel their conscience being stirred, or an intuition stops them doing something, it may well be they are sensing the desire of their guardians to keep them on the right track! (17:13–14; 41:46; 45:15).

H

Hadd ▶ see **hudud**.

Hadith (*had-eeth*) literally, news, report, account. The sayings, action or silent approval of the Prophet, the second source of information for Muslims concerning the right way to live. Those who memorised hadith had to record also the **isnad** or chain of narration – stating from whom that saying came. Collections of sayings of the Prophet written down by his companions during his lifetime or by their immediate successors are called *sahifas*. The earliest surviving work on hadith is the Muwatta of **Imam** Malik (d.795). Six collections are regarded as **sahih** or fully authentic – those of Imam Muhammad al-Bukhari (which lists 2,762) and Imam Muslim ibn al-Hajjaj (which lists 4,000), Abu Dawud, Tirmidhi, ibn Majah, and an-Nasa'i; other reliable collections are those of Darimi, Darqutni, Ibn Hanbal and Ibn Sa'd.

Hadith qudsi (*had-eeth kud-see*) from *qudus* meaning 'holy', these are sayings from Allah to the Prophet that are not part of the Qur'an. The Prophet did not learn or recite them like the **ayahs**, but used his own words and expressions to tell them.

Hafiz (*haf-eez*) pl. huffaz (*hu-faz*), a person who has learned the entire Qur'an by heart.

Hafsah (*haf-saah*) the daughter of **Umar**, and the fourth wife of the Prophet. When the Qur'an was written down, it was given into her safekeeping.

Hajar (*haj-aar*) the Egyptian wife of the **prophet Ibrahim** and the mother of his firstborn son **Isma'il**. ▶ See also **sa'y**.

Hajj (*ha-j*) the pilgrimage to the **Ka'bah** in **Makkah** and the nearby **Mount Arafat**, during the 8th to the 13th of the month of **Dhul-Hijjah**, the 12th month of the Islamic **calendar**. All Muslims are required to try to perform this duty once in their lifetime (▶ see **five pillars of Islam**), provided they have the means to do so, and are physically and mentally fit. Other conditions are that their funds must be honestly acquired, they should not be in debt, and their dependants should be cared for in their absence. Muslims who have grown old without being able to perform hajj, as long as they have a genuine excuse and did indeed have every **intention** of going, may pay for another person to go instead, or make a donation of the equivalent amount in **sadaqah** to some charity. This then counts as their own hajj. A pilgrim who has performed the hajj

The hajj – arriving at the Ka'bah, the stand at Mount Arafat, and stoning the jamarat.

is known as a hajji (masc.) or hajjah (fem.) (2:158, 196–203; 3:97; 5:3; 22:26–33). ▶ See also **Ibrahim, ihram, jamarat, Mina, miqat, Muzdalifah, tawaf, wuquf.**

Halal (*haa-lal*) literally, 'allowed'. The concept of halal does not only apply to **food laws**. That which God allows must be good for us, kind, and so on. Harmful deeds and things are always **haram**. (2:173; 5:4).

Hamd (*ham-d*) literally, praised, glory, glorification. The word is included in the name **Muhammad** meaning 'the praised one' and the phrase 'al-hamdu-li-Llah' (*al-ham-doo-lil-laah*) meaning 'praise be to Allah' (the equivalent of 'thanks be to God' and a polite form of response for Muslims when something good happens).

Hanif (*han-eef*) a devout person, one who believed in one true God in an age before the **revelation** of the Qur'an, when it was normal to worship many gods and **idols**.

Haqiqah (*haa-kee-kaa*) inner reality, truth, science of the 'inward'. The word is from *haqqa*, meaning to be true, right, just, valid.

Haram (*ha-raam*) an action or substance which is forbidden because it is harmful (2:173; 5:4).

Haram Sharif (*ha-raam sha-reef*) the Noble Sanctuary – the Grand Mosque in **Makkah** which

encompasses the **Ka'bah**, the hills of Safa and Marwah, and the well of **Zamzam**.

Harun (*ha-roon*) the prophet Aaron, brother and spokesman of **Musa** (19:53). His grave is on Mt Hor (Jabal Harun) near Petra in Jordan (see Bible, Numbers 20:22–9). The Qur'an presents him as a sincere **prophet** who discouraged his people from worshipping the golden idol of a calf. (7:150; 20:94).

Haya (*hi-yaa*) modesty in clothing, manners and way of life.

Heaven ▶ see **Paradise**.

Hell the place of **punishment** in the afterlife, described as a terrible, scorching, place of torment, sorrow and remorse (e.g. 14:16–17; 38:55–8; 43:74–6; 56:42–4). The descriptions are detailed, but most scholars interpret them symbolically. The idea of harsh punishment seems hard to reconcile with God's mercy, but it is clear that no one will be condemned to Hell unless absolutely resolved on self-destruction. (16:61; 92:14–16). ▶ See also **Akhirah**.

Hidden Imam the **Shi'ites** divided into two major branches, according to whether they believed in seven or twelve **imams**. In each group, it is claimed that the last imam mysteriously disappeared without dying, and lives on in a mystical way, guiding the faithful in their times of need. He will reappear one day to establish righteous rule at the time which will see the end of the world. ▶ See also **Mahdi**, **Seveners**, **Twelvers**.

Hijab (*hi-jab*) literally, barrier, cover, veil. The original hijab was a curtain which the Prophet put up to separate an area in his wives' houses where they could be private (33:53). The hijab of women's clothing is modest dress, which prevents the outline of the female body from being visible and reduces sexual temptation between men and women who are not intending to be marriage partners (▶ see **clothing – rules of modesty**). Inner hijab refers to the attitude of modesty (▶ see **haya**), the **intention** not to arouse (24:30–31; 33:59). Regarding these two aspects of hijab, one is meaningless without the other.

A typical form of hijab head-veil.

Hijrah (*hij-raah*) literally, departure, exit. The emigration of the Prophet and his companions from **Makkah** to **Madinah**. The year, 622 CE, is regarded as Year 1 in the Muslim **calendar**.

Hikmah (*hik-maah*) the concept of wisdom and tact, dealing tactfully with people.

Holy war ▶ see **jihad**.

Homosexuality sexual relations between members of the same sex. This is forbidden in Islam. (26:165–6; 4:16–18). ▶ See **zinah**.

Hospitality generous behaviour towards guests and visitors – one of the key Muslim virtues. Muslims should be generous to all people, no matter whether Muslim or non-Muslim. If a guest arrives, it is considered polite to offer full hospitality for a period of up to three days. After that, guests must take care not to linger on, in case their host may have difficulties in providing for them. (2:254, 261, 274).

Hudud (*hu-dood*) plural of hadd, literally, 'limits'. It refers to the limits imposed by Allah for **haram** and **halal**, and usually refers to the specific fixed penalties laid down in the Qur'an for particular crimes such as **theft** and **zinah**. (5:41; 17:32; 24:2–5).

Hunting in Islam, to allow any living thing to be misused for 'pleasure' is prohibited. Hunting, therefore, cannot be merely for sport. The purpose of taking the life of an animal must be to eat it, or get some other benefit from it. Anything killed without just cause will have to be accounted for on **Judgement Day**. Weapons used for hunting should be those that pierce or are sharp, such as arrows, knives, spears or bullets, and not blunt instruments such as clubs or stones. Creatures such as dogs and hawks are considered as natural hunters but, if used, they should be trained to hunt with skill and efficiency to avoid unnecessary suffering. Hunting is totally forbidden for those in the state of **ihram** (5:2, 98).

Hussein the second son of the Prophet's daughter **Fatimah** and **Ali**.

He refused to acknowledge Yazid the son of **Mu'awiyah** as **caliph**, and fought him in 681 at the battle of **Karbala**. Hussein was defeated and killed. The day of mourning on the 10th **Muharram** is held in his honour in the **Shi'ah** community. ▶ See **Ashurah**.

Hypocrite in Arabic, munafiq (*mu-naa-feek*) – a person who is pretending, claiming to be what they are not. According to Islam, it may be possible to fool one's fellow humans, but it is never possible to fool God. (2:9–20, 44; 9:64–5).

Ibadah (*ee-ba-daah*) worship, from **abd**, 'servant'. This is the concept of servanthood, being a servant of God. It does not just mean **prayer**, but includes any permissible action with the **intention** of serving Allah.

Iblis (*ib-lees*) ▶ see **Shaytan**.

Ibrahim (*ib-raa-heem*) a tribal sheikh from Ur in Mesopotamia (Iraq), who became known as al-Khalil (*al-kaa-leel*) 'the friend' (of God). Called by Allah to reject the **idol** worship of his tribe, he smashed

its statues to prove they were powerless (21:51–71). Under Allah's guidance, he then left his homeland to spend the rest of his life as a wandering nomad. He prayed for the gift of a good son, and his Egyptian wife, **Hajar**, gave birth to **Isma'il** (37:100–101). His other wife, Sarah, was childless. Idol-worshippers had offered animal and human **sacrifices** as attempts to please or 'bribe' their gods, and one night Ibrahim dreamed that Allah wanted him to sacrifice Isma'il as proof of his obedience. He told

Isma'il, and they both agreed to submit to what they thought was God's will. However, just as he was about to kill Isma'il, Allah stopped him and revealed that Ibrahim had already proved his obedience long ago (37:102–107). A ram was slaughtered instead, and this event is commemorated every year with **Id-ul-Adha**, at the time of the **hajj**. Allah then granted a son, Ishaq (*ee-shak*) (Isaac), to Ibrahim's barren wife, Sarah. (32:112).

Id (*eed*) Arabic word for a celebration repeated regularly, as opposed to a single event such as a wedding or a party for the birth of a child. All Muslims keep two main festival days, **Id-ul-Adha** and **Id-ul-Fitr**, and many also celebrate **Maulid an-Nabi**, **Ashurah**, **Laylat-ul-Miraj**, **Laylat-ul-Bara'at**, and **Laylat-ul-Qadr**. The usual greeting on these festivals is 'Id Mubarak' (*eed moo-baar-ak*), meaning 'the blessings of Id to you'.

An Id card.

Iddah (*id-daah*) the period of time a woman must wait before remarrying after **divorce** (three months) or after **mourning** the death of her husband (four months and ten days), to ensure that there is no confusion about who is the father of children born after these events. A pregnant woman's iddah finishes as soon as her child is born. (2:228–35; 33:49; 65:4–7).

Idols statues or objects which either in themselves represent 'gods' or powers of nature, or are regarded as places or 'focal points' where those powers might dwell. 360 such objects were said to have been placed in the **Ka'bah** before the Prophet cleansed it and restored it to the worship of the one true God.

Id prayer the special **prayer** for **Id** in which the whole Muslim community, including women and children, tries to join together. Small **mosque** communities may link up for this prayer. Large communities sometimes take over open fields, parks or large car-parks, as the numbers may run into thousands. It usually takes place an hour after sunrise; for large communities the Id prayers may be repeated several times during the feast day.

Id-ul-Adha (*eed-ul-ad-haa*) also known as Id-ul-Kabir (*eed-ul-kab-eer*), the 'great festival' of Islam, and, in Turkey, Qurban bayram (*koor-ban bai-ram*), the 'feast of sacrifice'. It takes place on the 10th of the lunar month **Dhul-Hijjah**, and ends the period of **hajj**. All Muslims celebrate it, whether on hajj or not. In Muslim countries it is a four-day holiday. It commemorates the willingness of the **prophet Ibrahim** to **sacrifice** his firstborn son **Isma'il**'s life, and Ismail's own willingness to lay down his life for God. Muslims who do not sacrifice an animal (or purchase one sacrificed for them) may pay the equivalent to charity.

Id-ul-Fitr (*eed-ul-fit-er*) this is the 'minor' festival of Islam, but it is enthusiastically celebrated because it marks the new moon at the end of the month-long self-denial and **fast** of **Ramadan**. People wear new clothes and give presents to children. It is also called Id-ul-Saghir (*eed-ul-sa-reer*) or 'little Id' and, in Turkey, Sheker bayram (*shek-er bai-ram*) or 'sugar festival'.

Iftar (*if-taar*) breakfast. The word usually refers literally, not to the first meal of the day, but to the meal that ends the day's **fasting** during **Ramadan**, at sunset.

Ihram (*ih-raam*) the state of purity entered by **hajj** pilgrims. This is symbolised for men by the wearing of two simple white cloths and for women by clothing covering the whole body apart from the face and hands. Clothing often indicates a person's status, **wealth** or occupation – all these are set aside in this reminder that people are equal before Allah, whether they be royalty or roadsweepers. The ihram cloths, like shrouds, also remind people of the mortality of their bodies, and the **life after death** of the **soul**. In the state of ihram, pilgrims must not be arrogant or impatient; marry, get engaged, or indulge in sexual activity; use perfume; carry weapons, kill or harm living things; break or uproot plants; wear shoes that cover the ankles; cut their hair or clip their nails. Men must not cover their heads; women must not cover their faces. The ihram rules are aimed at encouraging the pilgrim to set aside the cares and pleasures of this world in order to concentrate on Allah, but at the same time to feel love for God's **creation** and unity with it in acknowledgement that everything belongs to Allah. They also express purity, modesty, trust, simplicity, humility, non-aggression and gentleness. (5:3).

Pilgrim dressed in ihram cloths.

Ihsan (*ih-saan*) awareness of God – the conviction of a person who truly believes that God, though invisible, sees everything they do and knows every **intention** in their minds and hearts.

Ijma (*ij-maa*) the agreement of religious scholars when providing legal opinions on subjects not directly ruled upon in the Qur'an.

Ijtihad (*ij-ti-haad*) literally, 'to struggle', 'to make the utmost effort'. This refers to the exercise of reason in order to try and find an appropriate ruling on a matter not directly ruled upon in the Qur'an. The term applies to making use of principles, similarities and comparisons.

Ikhlas (*ik-laas*) sincerity. This describes the quality of a person who consciously does everything in life for the sake of Allah alone.

Imam (*im-aam*) in **Sunni** Islam, the imam is not a priest, but simply a respected person who leads the **prayers**. Circumstances and convenience have sometimes led to imams being employed and paid, but this is not the ideal. Any person who has a good knowledge of Islam and is of good character can act as imam, and anyone who knows the prayer can lead it. Women do not lead if there is a man available, but they may lead other women and children. In **Shi'ite** Islam, the imam is the supreme leader and, as a descendant of the Prophet, is considered to have special supernatural guidance so that his words are infallible. ▶ See also **Ayatollah**, **madhhab**.

Iman (*im-aan*) the word is from *amana*, to believe, and *amina*, to be tranquil in heart and mind, to be safe or secure, to trust, to have a serene confidence. Iman means 'faith', to consciously apply the principles of Islam so that acceptance of the will of Allah governs every action and **niyyah**.

Inheritance the leaving of property and money after death is subject to various rules in Islam, to ensure that people are provided for justly. Relatives receive set proportions. Personal preferences or hostilities can play almost no part: only a small proportion of one's property may be left to individually chosen causes. (2:180–82, 240; 4:7–9, 11–12, 19, 33, 176; 5:109–11).

Injil (*in-jeel*) this means 'gospel', but not in the same sense as the Gospels according to Saints Matthew, Mark, Luke and John which are included in the present **Christian** New Testament. It is the pure, unadulterated message from Allah revealed to the **prophet Isa** – not the human attempts to record the message many years later.

Innovation ▶ see **bidah**.

Insha Allah (*in-sha al-laah*) literally, 'if God wills'. This is a phrase used by Muslims when they have just mentioned a future plan or **intention**, e.g. 'I'll go tomorrow – if God wills'. After all, no one knows if it is God's will they should be alive tomorrow! (18:23).

Intention ▶ see **niyyah**.

Interest on money ▶ see **riba**.

Iqamah (*ik-aa-mah*) the second call to **prayer**, carried out not from the **minaret** but from inside the **mosque**, when the **imam** gets the people to stand up in their rows ready to start the prayer. ▶ See **adhan**.

Iqra! (*ik-raa*) meaning 'Recite!', this is the first word of the **revelation** given to the Prophet. Muslims believe the first revealed words to be **surah** 96:1–5, followed by surah 48:3.

Isa this is the Arabic name for Jesus. The Qur'an tells how he was miraculously born of the Virgin Mary, but does not deduce that this made him a 'son of God' (3:47). Neither do Muslims believe that Jesus died to save us from our sins as a **sacrifice**, redeemer or saviour, but that each one of us is responsible for our own sins (35:18). Muslims do however believe that Jesus was miraculously saved from death on the cross, and that he ascended into **Heaven** and will return again before the **end of the world** (▶ see **Mahdi**). Important Qur'anic passages referring to Jesus are 2:87; 5:46; 43:63; 57:27. ▶ See also **Injil, Maryam**.

Isha or salat-ul-isha (*saa-lat-ul-ish-shaa*) – the compulsory night **salah**, performed at some time during the hours of darkness, between one hour after sunset and whenever **fajr** starts.

Islam (*is-laam*) the true peace gained by willing submission to Allah's divine guidance. (3:85). ▶ See also **amal, din, ihsan, iman, taqwa**.

Isma'il the eldest son of the **prophet Ibrahim**.

Isma'ilis a **Shi'ite** sect that came into being after the death of the sixth **imam**, Ja'far as-Sadiq, in 765. ▶ See also **Seveners, Twelvers**.

Isnad (*is-naad*) the chain of transmission of a **hadith** carefully examined to check if it is reliable or not. Hadith that are not in keeping with the principles of the Qur'an are most probably well-meaning but not genuine.

Istanja (*is-tan-jaa*) washing the private parts after toilet. ▶ See **cleanliness**.

Istikhara (*is-ti-kaa-raa*) a special form of **trust**; a **prayer** of turning to Allah for guidance and direction over a particular problem, it involves trusting that the right thing to do will be made clear. It also involves submitting one's will entirely to that of Allah.

Itikaf (*it-tee-kaf*) seclusion from the world in order to concentrate on **prayer**. This is usually done during the last ten days of **Ramadan**. Men may stay at the **mosque**; women remain where they normally pray, in their houses – where family members play their part in supporting them by taking over from them all their normal duties.

J

Jahannam (*ja-ha-nam*) ▶ see **Hell**.

Jahiliyyah (*jaa-hil-ee-yaa*) the time of ignorance and superstition before the coming of Islam.

Jama'ah (*ja-ma-aah*) a gathering of people, a congregation. ▶ See also **Jumu'ah**.

Jamarat (*ja-ma-rat*) three stone pillars at **Mina** at which pilgrims on **hajj** hurl small stones, while promising to try to obey the will of God throughout the rest of their lives. This represents **Ibrahim** and his son **Isma'il** resisting the temptations of **Shaytan** three times.

Janaba (*ja-na-ba*) the state of being unclean, for which a person requires full ritual **ghusl**. To be *junub* is to be in the state of janaba – for example, after sexual intercourse.

Jannah (*jan-nah*) ▶ see **Paradise**.

Jerusalem the third most holy site of Islam after **Makkah** and **Madinah**. From around 1000 BCE it was the capital city of the Jewish people, captured from the Jebusites by the

Pilgrims stoning the pillar representing Shaytan.

prophet-king **Dawud** (David, Daud).
His son **Suleiman** built the temple to
the one true God there. Captured by
the Romans in 66 CE after the Jewish
Revolt, it was largely demolished
and **Jews** were banished from the
site. Places associated with **Isa**
become prominent after the
conversion of the Roman Emperor
Constantine to Christianity in the
fourth century. It was from
Jerusalem that the Prophet ascended
through the heavens on the **Laylat-
ul-Miraj**. The **Christian** Patriarch
handed the city over peacefully to
Caliph Umar. It was captured in 1095
by the Crusaders, who massacred
both Muslims and Jews, but in 1187
it was recaptured by the Muslims
under **Saladin**. The city was split
into Jewish and Muslim territory
when the State of Israel was
proclaimed in 1948, and has been in
Israeli hands since the Six-Day War
in 1967. Muslims are concerned that
the Jewish ambition to rebuild the
temple in Jerusalem will mean the
destruction of the **Dome of the Rock**
and the **al-Aqsa mosque**.

Jesus ▶ see **Isa**.

Jews the original **People of the
Book** (Arabic, Ahl al-Kitab), to
whom Allah granted a series of
revelations through chosen
prophets. However, Muslims do not
accept that any one race is chosen
above any other. In Islam, all races
are equal (5:20), and Muslims
honour all of God's prophets, unlike
the 'hard-hearted' peoples that
rejected them (4:153–61). The

prophets taught individual
responsibility and were opposed to
the ideas of 'priesthood' and a cult-
system based on **sacrifices**. Jews
who, before the time of Islam,
believed in one God and refused to
worship **idols** were regarded as
Muslims (▶ see **hanif**), and were
praised in the Qur'an (2:62; 4:162;
5:13; 26:197; 28:53). The Prophet
Muhammad hoped to convince the
Jews of **Madinah** of the truths of the
Qur'an (29:47) – he kept the **fast** of
Atonement at **Ashurah**, and the
original Muslim **prayer** had its
qiblah facing **Jerusalem** (2:142–4) –
but they rejected him. However, two
of the Prophet's wives were Jewish,
Safiyyah and Raihanah, both
widows of opponents defeated in
battle.

Jibril (*jib-reel*) the chief **angel** of
God; Jibril sometimes functions as
the means by which God sends
messages and **revelations** (2:97); and
was seen by **Ibrahim** and the Virgin
Mary (**Maryam**) as well as by the
Prophet **Muhammad** (69:38). Jibril is
frequently referred to in the Qur'an
as ruh al-Qudus, the holy spirit, or
ruh al-amin, 'the trustworthy spirit'
(17:85; 70:4; 97:4), the activator of
God's will, though not as part of the
godhead and in no sense the third
part of a Holy Trinity.

Jihad (*jee-haad*) this means self-
purification (29:6) – the word comes
from *juhd*, to strive, struggle, exert
oneself, be willing to fight for good
against **evil**. The great jihad is the
struggle against one's own base

inclinations (such as selfishness, lust, greed, pride, dishonesty). There is also the jihad in relation to **khilafah** – the struggle to act on behalf of Allah in caring for the planet and relieving suffering. This involves dedication to helping others, teaching, improving social conditions and so forth (49:15). Finally, there is the military sense of the word, which is much misused by Muslims and non-Muslims alike. A 'holy war' can only be in defence of the cause of Allah. It must be to restore peace or freedom of worship or freedom from **tyranny**; it must be led by a spiritual leader; and be fought only until the enemy lays down arms and asks for peace. The word jihad should not be used for wars of aggression or ambition, border disputes, national rivalries, the intent to conquer, suppress, colonise, exploit, or force people to accept a faith in which they do not believe. (2:190–93; 22:40; 41:34; 49:9).

Jinn (*jin*) elemental spirits, non-human beings created 'from fire' (in the same way that humans are created 'from humus' or earth). They are neither good nor **evil**, but can be either; and **surah** 72 mentions jinn that accepted Islam. They were created before humanity, as were the **angels**, and have **free will** like humans. They are not normally visible to humans, although humans are sometimes aware of them, or may experience the feeling of an atmosphere, perhaps malevolent, when they are nearby. The Prophet

said that they were attracted to places like deserts, ruins, and wherever humans and animals fulfilled their basic natural functions. The chief jinn is **Shaytan** or Iblis, who is always ill-willed towards humanity (because of his original jealousy), and tries to lure humans away from obedience to Allah. (6:100; 15:27; 34:41; 46:29–32; 55:15; 72:1–15; 114:4–6).

Jizya (*jiz-yaa*) the tax imposed on non-Muslims living under Muslim rule. ▶ See **Dhimmi**.

Job ▶ see **Ayyub**.

John the Baptist ▶ see **Yahya**.

Jonah ▶ see **Yunus**.

Judgement Day or Qayamah, the day of **resurrection** when, Muslims believe, all humans will discover their eternal fates: whether they will go to **Paradise** or to **Hell**. This will depend on our **intentions**, conscious and unconscious (16:61; 34:45), and on whether we have shown **repentance**. Our 'books' recorded by our **angels** are shown to us, so that we will be in no doubt of the justice of what we have earned. (17:13–14).

Jumu'ah (*ju-ma-aah*) Arabic name for Friday, the day when Muslims try to meet for **salat-ul-Jumu'ah** (62:9). If they do not attend, they may still perform salat-ul-**zuhr**. Although shops close during the time people are in the **mosque** in Muslim countries, Friday is not regarded as a 'day of rest'. The Qur'an teaches that Allah never rests. (2:255).

Juz (*jooz*) the Qur'an is 'divided' into 30 sections for the purposes of study and reading during the **tarawih prayers** of **Ramadan**. Each section is called a juz.

Congregational prayer.

Ka'bah (*ka-aa-baah*) the cube-shaped shrine at **Makkah** in the Great **Mosque**, the place towards which all Muslims turn when saying their **salah prayers**. The word Ka'bah means 'cube'. In the Muslim tradition, this was the site of the first shrine built for God on earth by the first human, **Adam**. It has been repaired many times, all later shrines being rebuilt on the same foundations. At the time of the Prophet it was no longer dedicated to the one true God but had become

a central shrine for some 360 **idols** and cult objects. The Prophet cleansed it, destroyed the idols, and re-established the worship of Allah.

Kaffarah (*kaf-faa-raah*) a 'covering' action made by someone who has made a mistake or committed a sin. It could be a gift of money or food to the poor, or **fasting**, or extra **prayers**.

Kafir (*ka-fir*) literally, 'one who covers up'; pl. kuffar or kafirun. This is an unbeliever, a person who does not believe in the one true God, and feels no sense of gratitude to or **trust** in a divine creator. ▶ See **kufr**.

Kalimah (*kaa-li-maah*) the 'word' or declaration of faith. ▶ See **shahadah**.

Karbala (*kaar-bal-aa*) the site of the battle between the Prophet's grandson **Hussein** and his rival Yazid. It is also where Hussein is buried, and a major shrine in Iraq.

Khadijah (*kad-ee-jaah*) the first wife of the Prophet, and his only wife for 25 years. He never remarried while she lived, and so we have two **sunnahs** – that of monogamy and, in different circumstances, that of multiple marriage. Neither **polygamy** nor monogamy is considered by Muslims right for its own sake. Khadijah was a wealthy and noble lady, twice widowed, with experience as a merchant when she employed the youthful **Muhammad** to trade for her in Syria. When he was 25, and she in her early forties, she proposed marriage to him, and despite their age difference it was a famous love-match. They had six children (▶ see **Prophet's family**). She was the Prophet's first **convert** and his staunch supporter during all his times of **persecution**. She became ill during the three years when Muslims were boycotted by the clans, and died in 620 at the age of 64. The Prophet never ceased to miss her, until he died 12 years later. He once said to **Aishah**: 'She believed in

me when no one else did; she accepted Islam when people rejected me; and she helped and comforted me when there was no one else to help me.'

Khalid (*kaa-lid*) originally an enemy of Islam, and a leading officer against the Muslims in many battles, he became a **convert** to Islam after the conquest of **Makkah**. The Prophet assured him that his conversion wiped out all his past. This essential principle for all converts to Islam signified spiritual birth and was the way to bring peace.

Kharijites (*kar-ee-jites*) an early group of Muslims that had its origins in the dispute between **Ali** and **Mu'awiyah**. One of the Kharajites killed Ali. Small groups still remain within the Arab world.

Khilafah (*kil-aa-faah*) the concept of taking responsibility or ruling in God's name. It refers to many aspects of life – care of the planet, looking after one's family and dependants, and taking action to improve and protect a whole variety of conditions of life. ▶ See **caliph**.

Khitan (*kit-aan*) the removal of the foreskin of the penis. Allah commanded the **prophet Ibrahim** that this should be done for all male Muslims thereafter (Genesis 17:10). It is usually done when the infant is around a week old, or a little later if the baby is not strong (2:124). In Turkey, boys may be circumcised as late as nine or ten, but most Muslims regard this as wrong. Female circumcision, still practised in the Sudan and lower Egypt, is a tradition that pre-dates both Islam and Christianity, and is condemned by both.

Khul (*kul*) the **divorce** of a husband by a wife. She applies to a judge, presenting her reasons, and often gives up some (or all) of the **dowry** she received on her marriage.

Khulwah (*kool-waah*) privacy, a man and woman being alone together in a place where there is no fear of intrusion by anyone else, so that an opportunity exists for sexual intimacy. In Islam, only the members of the woman's immediate family are allowed to be in privacy with her. This rule is not based on lack of **trust**, but is intended to protect the woman. (24:31; 33:35).
▶ See also **mahrem**.

Khums (*kooms*) the contribution (additional to **zakah**) of a fifth of their surplus income, paid by **Shi'ah** Muslims. **Sunni** Muslims only apply it to booty from warfare.

Khutbah (*koot-baa*) a sermon or speech. The word usually refers to the two sermons (now generally preached in Arabic and in the normal language of the community) given before the Friday **prayer**.

Kitab (*ki-tab*) the book, i.e. the Qur'an.

Kufr (*koo-fer*) literally, to cover up, to reject. The act of declaring disbelief. An unbeliever is a **kafir**. In the Qur'an the word refers to **idol**-worshippers and atheists.

Kunya name (*koon-yaa*) the practice of a parent taking the name of a child; for example, when Ahmed and Laila have a child, Hussein, Ahmed becomes Abu Hussein and Laila is Umm Hussein.

Kursi (*koor-see*) **1** a throne or chair, usually referring to the carved wooden stand on which the Qur'an is placed; **2** the name of a famous verse of the Qur'an, the 'verse of the throne', or ayat-al-kursi. (2:255).

A wooden stand for the Qur'an.

Last Prophet Muslims do not think that the Prophet **Muhammad** was the founder of Islam, or that Allah was a different God from the one worshipped by **Jews** and **Christians**. The will of Allah has always been revealed through special chosen people; the Prophet was the last in a very long 'chain' of messengers (3:84; 5:86, etc.). Muhammad was, however, given his message in a particular and unique way – a series of **revelations** which were remembered and collected up and written down word for word. Since his time 1,400 years ago, there has been no other **prophet** offering revelation of God's will in the same prophetic 'chain'. Muslims believe, therefore, that the Prophet Muhammad was the 'seal' of all previous prophets, and that he was the last.

Laylat-ul-Bara'at (*lay-lat-ul-ba-raat*) the 'Night of Blessing' or 'Night of the Decree', this is celebrated on the 14th Shabaan, the night of the full moon in the month before **Ramadan**, when the Prophet used to begin his preparations for Ramadan by passing whole nights in prayer. Many Muslims stay up reading the Qur'an all night. On the 15th they may visit the **graves** of departed loved ones, to pray for their **souls**. The 'Decree' refers to the belief that on this night Allah decrees the fates of certain people – making it known to the **angels** which person will live and which will die; whose sins will be forgiven and who will be condemned.

Laylat-ul-Miraj (*lay-lat-ul-mir-raaj*) the 'Night of Ascent', usually celebrated on the 27th Rajab, when the Prophet was summoned from his sleep and taken to **Jerusalem**, from where he ascended through the heavens to the throne of God (17:1). This is so unlike the other records of the Prophet's life that the opinion of Muslim scholars is divided as to whether it was a miraculous event, a trance or a vision. As he and **Jibril** rose through the heavens, they saw other **prophets**, including **Musa**, **Ibrahim**, **Yahya** and **Isa**, and prayed with them. It was as a result of their discussion with Musa that the number of times per day Muslims should pray was fixed at five. Neither the Prophet nor the **angel** could approach close to the throne of God, which was surrounded by brilliant light. This experience occurred shortly after the Prophet's loss of his wife **Khadijah**, and his uncle **Abu Talib**. It brought him fresh hope and vigour. ▶ See also **al-Aqsa**.

Laylat-ul-Qadr (*lay-lat-ul-kad-er*) the 'Night of Power', when the Prophet received the first **revelation** of the Qur'an (97:1–5), this is therefore the most important night in Islam. The date is not certain; all that is known is that it fell on one of the odd-numbered dates during the last ten days of **Ramadan**. It is frequently observed on the 27th. Many Muslims stay up all night at the **mosque**, reading the Qur'an. Some Muslims make absolutely sure of not missing the night by spending (if they can without depriving or inconveniencing others) the entire last ten days at the mosque. ▶ See also **itikaf**.

Lian (*lee-an*) if a husband accuses his wife of **zinah** without witnesses, they each have to swear four times that what they say is true, and the fifth oath brings a curse on themselves if they are lying. If the wife swears a fifth time that she is innocent, she will not be condemned to the hadd punishment (▶ see **hudud**), but the couple are irrevocably **divorced**, and can never remarry. (24:6–9).

Life after death ▶ see **Akhirah**.

M

Madhhab (*math-hab*) a 'school' of religious law, or a system of **fiqh**. Four madhhabs (the correct plural is madhahib) have been accepted as authoritative by **Sunni** Muslims: the Hanafi (from Abu Hanifa, 669–767), the Maliki (from Malik ibn Anas, 717–95), the Shafi'i (from al-Shafi'i, 767–820) and the Hanbali (from Ahmad ibn Hanbal, d.855). **Shi'ite** Muslim groups developed their own system of law and moral precepts from their sixth imam, Jafar al-Sadiq (d.765). Most Muslims still follow one or other of these schools, but although these eminent teachers are so highly venerated, their authority is not considered to be beyond question.

Madinah (*ma-dee-naah*) the town of Yathrib whose inhabitants invited the Prophet to leave **Makkah** and come there to rule. In his honour, it took the name Madinat-al-Nabi (the town of the Prophet), or Madinah for short. ▶ See **Ansar**, **Hijrah**, **Muhajirun**.

Madrassah (*ma-dra-saah*) the **mosque** school, where Muslims learn how to recite and understand the Qur'an, how to carry out Muslim practices, and the general principles of Islam. Many youngsters in the UK attend madrassah for around two hours every day, after their normal schooling.

Maghreb (*mur-reb*) Arabic name for the West. It usually refers to the Muslim countries of North Africa – Morocco, Algeria, Libya and Tunisia – although Western countries with the fastest growing number of **converts** are now the USA, the UK and parts of Europe.

Maghrib or salat-ul-maghrib (*saa-lat-ul-mur-rib*) – the compulsory **salah** performed any time from the moment just after the sun sinks until the fall of darkness. It is forbidden to pray at the exact moment of sunset, for fear of any association with sun-worship.

Magic in Arabic, sifr (*sif-er*). This does not mean 'doing tricks', but trying to predict and influence the future by the use of horoscopes, **divination**, astrology, omens and so forth. In Islam it is counted as a deadly sin (2:102). At the time of the Prophet numerous mediums, diviners and soothsayers claimed special powers through contact with

elemental spirits or **jinn**, and other secret sources. Those who seek such powers not only commit **shirk** but are being tricked by **evil** entities. The Qur'an states that whatever these sources reveal is based on falsehood and cruel delusion, for Allah alone knows the future. (5:93–4; 7:188; 10:107; 27:65; 34:14; 35:2).

Mahdi (*maa-dee*) Muslims believe the Madhi to be an **imam** who will rule over the world before **Judgement Day**. He will defeat the **dajjal**. Some think the Madhi may be the **prophet Isa**, who ascended to **Heaven** and will return to earth to fight the Anti-Christ (4:159). **Shi'ah** Muslims believe that the Mahdi is the **Hidden Imam**, who disappeared from earth in mysterious circumstances, but who will reappear to usher in the final years before the **end of the world**. ▶ See also **Seveners**, **Twelvers**.

Mahrem (*maah-rem*) a member of the opposite sex whose closeness by marriage or blood ties means they are allowed to be in private with you. A woman's mahrem are her husband, father, grandfather, son, brother, uncle or nephew. (33:55). ▶ See also **khulwah**.

Makkah (*mak-kaah*) the city in Saudi Arabia where the Prophet was born, and where the **Ka'bah** is located. The place to which all Muslims turn for **qiblah** when they pray, and the place of pilgrimage on the **hajj**. Its original name was Bakkah.

The Ka'bah shrine in the Great Mosque at Makkah.

Makruh (*mak-rooh*) an action –
such as **divorce** – which is
disapproved of in Islamic law, but
not actually forbidden.

Male supremacy the Qur'an
makes it very clear that to Allah male
and female are equal **souls** and of
equal value; however, because of the
many extra pains and physical
weaknesses women suffer, it is
expected that a good Muslim man
will take care of and protect his
womenfolk; he therefore has a
position of great responsibility which
is not to be abused by **tyranny**. (4:34).

Mamelukes (*mam e-looks*)
descendants of Turkish and
Circassian slave-soldiers who
became military rulers in Egypt. The
most famous was Baybars (d.1277),
who drove the **Crusaders** out of

Syria and halted the **Mongol**
advance. As a result of their success,
Cairo became the centre of the
Islamic world, and the al-Azhar
university the most important seat of
orthodox Islamic learning. The
Mameluke dynasty lasted from 1250
to 1517 CE, when it was defeated by
the **Ottomans**.

Mandub (*man-doob*) an action
which is recommended in Islam, but
not compulsory; this includes any
aspect of the Prophet's personal
example – e.g. **hospitality**.

Maqam Ibrahim (*ma-kam ib-raa-
heem*) the large rock upon which the
prophet Ibrahim is said to have
stood while directing the rebuilding
of the **Ka'bah** (2:125). These days it is
protected by a glass dome.

Marabout (*mar-a-boo*) a holy man, saintly person. In some Islamic cultures the **grave** of such a person is guarded with great devotion, but many Muslims disapprove of this because it runs the risk of a form of **shirk** – **prayers** being offered to the marabout to grant requests of fertility and so on, instead of praying to Allah.

Marriage a contract involving rights and responsibilities between a man and woman. Successful marriages are not 'made in **Heaven**' but are the result of a great deal of **tolerance**, hard work and good will. Many marriages are arranged by the parents of young people (▶ see **arranged marriages**, **nikah**). Muslim males may marry **Christian** or Jewish (▶ see **Jews**) women, but Muslim women are expected to marry Muslim men. If either partner breaks the contract terms, or denies the rights of the other, **divorce** is permitted. (4:22–4; 5:6).

Maryam (*mar-i-yam*) the Muslim name for the Virgin Mary, the mother of the **prophet Isa**. She is mentioned frequently in the Qur'an, where she is also called the 'daughter of Imran', acknowledging her Levitical descent from the father of **Musa** (3:35). Her purity, nobility and innocence, and her role as mother of the Messiah Isa, is never questioned. When she saw the **angel Jibril** and asked how it was possible that she could be pregnant, never having 'known a man', she was told that Allah has only to say 'Be' and it

is so (3:47). Muslims accept the Virgin Birth of Isa without drawing the conclusion that this made him a 'son of God' in the **Christian** sense. No miracle is beyond God's power. (3:35–51; 4:156; 19:16–33; 21:98; 66:12).

Masjid (*mas-jid*) from *sujud*, to prostrate or bow down, this means literally a 'place of prostration'. The Prophet said that one could pray in any clean place, thus making it a masjid. He said: 'Wherever the hour of prayer overtakes you, you shall perform it. That place is a **mosque**.' Allah can be worshipped anywhere, and the most important place of worship is the heart. Some mosques are extremely simple, others very grand. Some Muslims feel it is right to dedicate the very best of buildings to Allah; others prefer to avoid any show of ostentation or the spending of lavish sums on elegant buildings.

Maulid an-Nabi (*maw-leed an-naa-bee*) a celebration of the birth of the Prophet, which was probably on 20th August, 570 CE. In the Muslim **calendar** it is celebrated on the 12th Rabi al-Awwal. Some Muslims celebrate it with processions, special **prayers** and Qur'an readings, parties, and suchlike activities in honour of the Prophet. Others feel this is **bidah**, and disapprove of a festival that is in honour of a human being, not God.

Mihrab (*mih-raab*) a focal point or niche in the wall of the mosque that

shows the direction of **Makkah**.
► See **qiblah**.

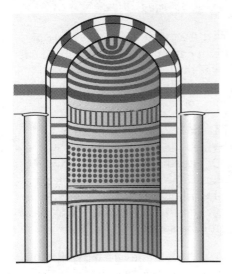

An ornamental mihrab.

Mina (*mee-naa*) the site of the place on the **hajj** route where pilgrims stay on the 10th–12th **Dhul-Hijjah**, and where they hurl pebbles at the **jamarat** (► see **Muzdalifah**). Mina is now joined to **Makkah** by modern walkways. It has some hotels for pilgrim accommodation, but most people camp out in tents.

Minaret (*min-aar-et*) a tall tower, used for the **adhan**.

Minbar (*min-baar*) a pulpit or raised platform from which the **imam** can deliver the **khutbah**.

Miqat (*mee-kaat*) this is the 'place appointed': the distance from **Makkah** at which an intending pilgrim must put on **ihram**. The miqat points are about 50 km (31 miles) to the east and west, and 250 km (155 miles) to the north and south of Makkah. Many pilgrims these days put on their white cloths before boarding planes. ► See **hajj**.

Moderation with reference to Islam this means doing one's best to follow Muslim principles and practices without intolerance or **extremism**.

Monasticism withdrawal from the world to live a life of self-denial, either alone or in a community. It usually involves giving up **sex** and suppressing the sexual urge. This is not approved of in Islam; as long as a person has the means to marry, dedication to the service or worship of Allah is unacceptable as an excuse for not marrying. Some of the Prophet's companions wished to relinquish **dunya**, to the extent of forsaking their wives and families and becoming like monks, but he ordered them not to do so. (5:90). ► See also **celibacy**.

Mongols hordes of these warriors from central Asia swept through the Islamic world in the 13th and 14th centuries. The most famous Mongol leaders were Genghis Khan (d.1241), his grandson Hulago, and Timur the Lame (Tamburlaine). Huge numbers of Muslims died, libraries and **mosques** were burnt to the ground and entire cities destroyed under their rule. When the **Caliph** of Baghdad was killed, Islam for the first time lost its ruler. The Mongols were eventually defeated by Baybars the **Mameluke**. Eventually the Mongols were converted to Islam, but ironically the name of Islam has suffered from being associated with the bloodthirsty reputation earned by the Mongols in their raids against Muslims.

Moors the Muslims of Spain who originated from Morocco.

Moses ▶ see **Musa**.

Mosque ▶ see **masjid**.

Mount Arafat the small mountain on the plain of Arafat, a few kilometres from **Makkah**. It was here that **Adam** and Hawwah were reunited and forgiven their sins. Now the scene of the climax of the **hajj**, the **wuquf** on the 9th **Dhul-Hijjah**, when pilgrims gather to pray and ask for **forgiveness**.

Mourning grief for a person who has died. Muslims are expected to have faith in God and **Akhirah**, a future life to come after the **death** of the body. Therefore too much grief is frowned on, and the custom in some societies for women to weep and wail loudly is in fact forbidden. A widow may mourn a husband for four months and ten days (2:234), but in all other cases three days is **sunnah**. Relatives and friends should always support the bereaved person and give practical help whenever they can. ▶ See also **rawdah**.

Mu'adhin (*mu-aa-theen*) also called *muezzin*. This is the person

who makes the call to prayer. The first such caller was the Abyssinian ex-slave, **Bilal**.

Mu'awiyah (*mu-aa-wee-yaa*) the fifth **caliph**, son of Abu Sufyan. He was the first of the **Ummayyad** caliphs, whose dynasty ruled from 661 to 750 CE.

Mubah (*mu-bah*) an action for which there is no ruling in the Qur'an, but which is left up to the conscience of the individual; e.g. should one smoke cigarettes, wear make-up or tell a white lie to avoid hurting someone's feelings?

Mughals (*mu-gals*) a dynasty of Muslim rulers in India.

Muhajirun (*mu-ha-ji-roon*) the 'Emigrants' – the Muslims who left all their possessions behind in **Makkah** and went with the Prophet to make their homes in **Madinah**.

Muhammad (*mu-ham-mad*) literally, 'the praised one'. The name of the man chosen by Allah to receive the Qur'an. Born in 570 CE, the Year of the Elephant, in **Makkah**. His father **Abdullah** died before he was born and his mother **Aminah** when he was only six. He was then raised by his grandfather **Abd al-Muttalib** and his uncle **Abu Talib** and became a shepherd and trader, famous for his honesty, kindness and sound judgement. At the age of 25 he married his employer, the widow **Khadijah**, and fathered six children by her. At the age of 40 he was called to be Allah's messenger and he received the **revelation** of the Qur'an over the next 23 years. Persecuted by his own people, he eventually left Makkah and became the ruler of **Madinah**. He captured Makkah in 630 without bloodshed. In 632 he died, in the arms of his youngest wife **Aishah**. May peace be upon him. ▶ See also **hamd**.

Muharram (*mu-ha-ram*) the first month in the Islamic **calendar**, this is one of the four months in which warfare is prohibited or **haram** (from which the name is derived). ▶ See also **Ashurah**.

Muhrim (*muh-reem*) a person in **ihram**.

Mujahideen (*mu-jaa-hid-deen*) warriors on **jihad** or 'holy war', those prepared to sacrifice their lives in the service of Allah. The name is frequently given to resistance fighters engaged in political struggles in Islamic areas of the world, e.g. Afghanistan and Iran.

Mujtahid (*muj-taa-heed*) a **Shi'ite** religious scholar.

Mullah (*mul-laah*) a teacher.

Mumin (*mu-meen*) literally, 'faithful'. This is someone who possesses **iman**, or deep faith and **trust** in God – a believer.

Munkar and Nadir (*mun-kaar, naa-deer*) the **angels** that question **souls** after **death**.

Musa (*mu-saa*) Arabic name for the **prophet Moses**, the chief prophet of the **Jews**. The Qur'an tells how he

was raised as an Egyptian prince, but called by the one true God to lead the Israelites out of slavery. He received the **revelation** known to Muslims as the **Tawrah**, the best-known part of which is the Ten Commandments. (2:51–61; 5:22–9; 6:84; 7:103–45; 10:75–92; 11:96–110; 17:101–3; 18:60–82; 19:51–3; 20:9–98; 23:45–9; 25:35–6; 26:10–69; 27:7–14; 28:4–42; 37:114–22; 40:23–46; 43:46–56; 51:38–40; 53:36; 79:15–26; 87:19).

Music only three categories of music are **haram** in Islam: that which encourages lust and uncontrolled sexual urges (much of modern pop music); that which incites nationalistic fervour (military music and themes like 'Rule Britannia'); and that which encourages people to show off and become conceited.

Muslim (*mus-leem*) any person who has accepted Islam by submitting his or her life to the will of Allah.

Muslim Brotherhood a reform movement started in Egypt by Hassan al-Banna in 1928. It demands total dedication to God, extreme religious discipline, and a refusal to compromise. Offshoots have tended to become extremist (▶ see **extremism**). The Muslim Brotherhood is particularly feared by Islamic countries whose governments have become lax, corrupt, or very westernised, or who wish to give a 'modern' interpretation to Islam.

Mutah (*mu-taah*) so-called 'temporary marriage'. Originally this was allowed by the Prophet as an honourable means for his warriors to satisfy their sexual urges when they were away from home, but it was soon revealed that this practice was unacceptable and insulting to women, and it was banned. It is still practised in some Islamic societies, notably in Iran, where some Muslim men claim that it is justified; but most women regard it as little more than permitted prostitution. (24:33).

Muzdalifah (*muz-daa-lee-faah*) the place where pilgrims on **hajj** collect 49 small pebbles to 'hurl at the **Devil'** (▶ see **jamarat**). After the **wuquf** at **Mount Arafat**, pilgrims make the **asr prayer**, and then head back towards **Makkah**, stopping at Muzdalifah for **maghrib** and **isha**.

Mysticism inner spiritual knowledge and awareness. In Islam, mysticism includes **Sufism**.

N

Nabi (*naa-bee*) a **prophet**, or messenger of God. A person who surrenders his or her entire being to Allah. This name is used mainly for prophets whose **revelation** from Allah was not left in a written form. ▶ See also **rasul**.

Nafs (*nafs*) meaning self, soul, mind, being, this word is connected to the word *nafusa*, to be precious or valuable. The concept of nafs includes a person's character, in terms of both inherited traits and conditioned behaviour. ▶ See also **ruh**.

Namaz (*nam-aaz*) the Urdu word for **salah**.

Names a Muslim's name should be honourable and encouraging, but not conceited or false. One should not name a Muslim infant 'beautiful one' or 'strong in generosity' because the child might turn out to be no such thing; and one should never use hurtful nicknames like 'fatty' or 'spotty'. The most generally favoured names are 'servant of God' names, which include the word **Abd** followed by one of the attributes or names of God (e.g. Rahman meaning 'mercy', or Karim 'beloved' – 7:180; 17:110; 20:8; 59:24). To use the name Abdul followed by **Muhammad** would be thought quite incorrect and an expression of **shirk**; and Abdul should not be followed by any other person's name either. The Prophet frequently changed people's names if he disapproved of them.

Nawafil (*na-wa-fil*) sing. *nafl*, meaning literally 'a gift'; a voluntary act of **ibadah**, for example, **prayers** over and above the **fard**.

Nazala (*na-za-la*) literally, 'sent down' – a message from Allah. The word is used over 200 times in the Qur'an to distinguish this from other forms of **revelation**.

Night of Ascent ▶ see **Laylat-ul-Miraj**.

Night of Power ▶ see **Laylat-ul-Qadr**.

Nikah (*nee-kaa*) the **marriage** ceremony, consisting of the reciting of **ayahs** from the Qur'an, the agreement to the terms of the **dowry**, the exchange of vows in front of witnesses, and the signing of the agreement to the specific details of the marriage contract. For example, if a bride does not wish to give permission for her husband to take more wives at any future time, it is sensible to make this clear in the nikah certificate. The bride does not have to have a special dress or even be present if she does not wish to, so long as she sends her **wali** and two genuine witnesses to her willingness to the marriage and its terms. The scarlet-and-gold dresses, henna pattern-painting and huge parties given by Asians are of cultural origin, and have nothing to do with Islam. The couple are legally married once the contract has been signed, but because of their age or personal circumstances they may decide not to live together until later.

Signing a marriage contract.

A **walimah** announces publicly that the couple are legally married and entitled to live together. In the UK, the registration may occur at any stage in this process, and if they register at a registry office, it is not necessary to have an **imam** present.

Nisab (*nee-saab*) the minimum amount of **wealth** – whatever form that wealth takes – from which **zakah** can be deducted.

Niyyah (*nee-yaah*) deliberate intention. In Islam, the intention of a person to do something is all-important, and in many cases counts as much as, or even more than, the action itself. If you intended to do a particular thing, but were prevented by circumstances (e.g. you intended to help a sick person, who died before you got there), it would count for you as if you had done it. If, on the other hand, you did a good deed by chance, without having had the intention of doing so, it would not count for you. Similarly, if you did a bad deed without meaning to (e.g.

you killed someone in an accident), it would not count against you.

Noah ▶ see **Nuh**.

Nudity appearing naked. This is disapproved of in Islam. Muslims value **haya**, even in intimate sexual relationships between husband and wife.

Nuh (*nooh*) one of the major named **prophets** in the Qur'an. He was called to warn a very corrupt society of a catastrophe to come if they did not change their ways. They refused to listen or believe and, in the end, they were wiped out by a great flood. Only the believers of Nuh's family were saved by a huge ship, or Ark, they had built (7:59–64). The main lesson here is the hard one that no one can influence God on behalf of anyone else – each person is responsible for his or her own judgement. A wife and son of Nuh refused to believe or enter the Ark, and consequently were drowned (11:45–7; 66:10).

O

Old age old people are valued in Islam for their **hikmah**, experience and **sabr**. Muslims have a duty to take care of their parents when that becomes necessary, in partial repayment for the care those parents took of them when they were young and helpless (17:23–4). Old people should always be treated with respect, even if their mental abilities are no longer clear and sharp. The Prophet once made an old lady cry when he told her there were no old people in **Heaven**; but he explained that all who went there were given renewed youth and vigour.

Oneness of God ▶ see **Tawhid**.

Organisations when people organise themselves in order to do good, it adds to individual strength. However, organisations can cause division, as when the underlying aim of a Muslim organisation is to be recognised as the 'best' way to 'represent' Islam in their society. The Prophet disapproved of anything that divided up the followers into cliques or groups, or prevented them from praying together. (2:176; 3:105).

Ottomans a dynasty of **caliphs** in Turkey. The last caliph was deposed in 1924 by Mustafa Kemal Ataturk, who set up a socialist republic. Since then there has been no caliph in Islam.

P

Pacifism the notion that it is always wrong to fight. Although Islam proclaims peace, Muslims are not total pacifists; they believe that there are certain circumstances in which it would be wrong *not* to

fight; for example to defend the weak, the oppressed and those persecuted for their religion.

Pan-Arabism the idea of unification of all Arab states into one

United Arab Republic (UAR) on the lines of the United States of America (USA) or the Union of Soviet Socialist Republics (USSR – now broken up). Problems include considering who might qualify – those who are born Arabs, or those for whom Arabic is the first language?

Pan-Islam the idea of the unification of all Muslim states. Many Muslims favour a return to the **Madinah** ideal, the creation of a kingdom of Islam, which would be led by a **caliph** and would include all Muslims, no matter what their nationality.

Paradise or Jannah, the Muslim name for Heaven; in the afterlife, the place of reward for those accepted and forgiven by Allah. It comes from the Persian word for garden, *paradisa*, and its imagery usually includes peaceful scenes of trees, plants and water – much cherished by inhabitants of land which would be desert unless artificially watered and cared for. Descriptions are given in detail in the Qur'an (e.g. 37:43–8; 38:50–52; 43:70–73; 48:5; 56:11–26), but most scholars take the point of view that these are to be interpreted symbolically, since the Qur'an states clearly that the true nature of the afterlife lies beyond human knowledge and understanding (32:17).

Pbuh this stands for 'peace be upon him', the words of respect added by Muslims when speaking about the Prophet **Muhammad**. Many Muslims also add this phrase when speaking of any other **prophet**, saint or noble companion of the Prophet Muhammad – male or female. Sometimes the letters 'saw' are added instead, standing for the Arabic version of the same phrase – salaam aleihim wa-salaam. Another version is 'saas' for salla Allahu alayhi wa-salaam – 'may the peace and blessing of Allah be upon him'.

People of the Book in Arabic, Ahl al-Kitab (*aal al-kit-ab*) – those (i.e. **Jews** and **Christians**) who, before the coming of the Prophet **Muhammad**, believed in the one true God through the **revelations** of the many earlier **prophets**. (3:64, 70; 29:46).

Persecution deliberate ill-treatment and abuse suffered by those who are disliked or unwanted for some reason they cannot help – e.g. for their race, culture or beliefs. The early Muslims faced persecution for their beliefs, often including physical torture and possible death, as well as ridicule and abuse. The Prophet set the example of acting with dignity when abused, and with **forgiveness** for his tormentors when he was in a position to do so. Islam is against all forms of persecution. (22:40).

Photographs these are allowed in Islam so long as they are not:
1 pornographic or stirring up lust;
2 idolatrous or stirring up leader-worship; 3 in any way encouraging

feelings that are contrary to Islam. Many Muslims do not display photographs of people or animals, just as they do not display paintings of them (▶ see **art**). Some tourist guidebooks say Muslims are afraid the photos will take their **souls**; but such fears are nothing to do with Islam. However, many Muslim women prefer not to have their images recorded by people outside their own family, even when fully dressed, as they do not know how the photograph will be used.

Pilgrimage setting out on a special journey with the **intention** to visit a particular holy place or shrine. ▶ See **hajj**.

Pilgrimage, the Final this refers to the only true **hajj** performed by the Prophet, the pilgrimage to **Makkah** after its capture, and the restoration of the **Ka'bah** to the worship of the one true God by people who were all committed Muslims. It was on this occasion that the Prophet gave his famous sermon. ▶ See **Sermon, the Last**.

Pillars of Islam ▶ see **five pillars of Islam**.

Polyandry the practice of a woman being able to marry more than one husband. This is forbidden in Islam, mainly because it is believed that a child has the right to know who its father is. In fact, societies usually have far more women than men without partners over the age of 35 (e.g. the USA has nearly 8 million

'surplus' older women, the UK around 4 million, Germany around 5 million). ▶ See also **polygamy**.

Polygamy the practice of **marriage** to more than one partner, usually taken to mean a man having more than one wife. This is allowed in Islam, on certain conditions: the man must have the certain knowledge that his first wife will not be hurt by the new marriage; he may not marry more than four wives; he must be able to deal justly with all of them (4:3). He should have sufficient financial resources to look after all their needs (and possible children), he must do equal justice to them all, and he must have enough energy to satisfy their physical needs (although this does not mean equal **sex**). Polygamy has been accepted as a solution to various social problems: the large numbers of widows and orphans left after a battle; a wife suffering from a serious illness such as paralysis, when she may appreciate a helper and is also sympathetic to her husband's physical needs; a wife becoming mentally ill, or so aged, weak and infirm that she cannot manage the household; a wife's character becoming unacceptable, or if she leaves Islam, or deserts the home and family (through no fault of her husband's); and if the husband has fallen desperately in love with someone else and the marriage with the first wife has broken down but she does not wish **divorce**. It is a gross abuse of Islam when men bend the rules in order to 'trade in an old model for a new one', or try to excuse their own moral weaknesses, or act cruelly.

Prayer the practice of speaking to God. Five daily prayers are regarded as compulsory (▶ see **salah**), and all other prayers are voluntary (▶ see **nawafil**) (20:130). A person's private requests and supplications to God for help and guidance are known as **du'a** prayers. Muslims believe that God's **angels** draw especially close to people when they are praying, and that some times of day are particularly blessed – for example, the end of the night, just before dawn. ▶ See also **rakah**.

Prayer of Light a famous prayer of the Prophet: 'O Lord! Illumine my heart with light, my sight with light and my hearing with light. Let there be light on my right hand and on my left, and light behind me, and light going before me.'

Prophecy in Arabic, risalah (*ri-saa-laah*) – the revealing of God's will to humanity. If God is to judge us on our actions and lives, then it is only fair that we are provided with the rules to guide us. Knowing what the will of God is, we may choose whether to obey it or not.

Prophet a person specially chosen by God to receive insights and messages, and pass them on for the guidance of humanity (▶ see **nabi**, **rasul**). When Muslims speak of 'the Prophet', they are referring to the Prophet **Muhammad.** ▶ See also **prophets in the Qur'an**.

Prophet's family the immediate family of the Prophet included his wife **Khadijah** and their six children (Qasim and Tayeb who died in infancy, Zainab, Ruqaiyyah, Umm Kulthum and **Fatimah**); his subsequent wives and son Ibrahim; his foster-sons **Ali** and Zaid ibn Haritha; the husbands and children of his daughters (especially Hassan and Hussein and Zainab – Fatimah's children – and Umamah, Zainab's daughter). Also included were his Bedouin wet-nurse Halimah, his childhood nurse Umm Aieman and, when she married his foster-son Zaid, their son Usamah.

Prophets in the Qur'an 25 are mentioned in the Qur'an by name, but Islam teaches that there were thousands sent before **Muhammad**. The 'major prophets' were **Nuh**, **Ibrahim**, **Musa**, **Suleiman** and **Isa**. Only three are not mentioned in the Bible: Hud, Salih and Shweib (the father-in-law of Musa). The full list is on page 80.

Prophet's wives there is some dispute over the exact number. Most contemporary books state that he had nine wives living when he died, which would mean that the Jewish Raihanah, and Maryam the Coptic **Christian** were only concubines or servant-wives (a status that was legal and commonplace before the coming of Islam). Other authorities maintain that these women definitely had the status of wife. Those who were certainly his wives were **Khadijah** bint Khuwailid, Sawdah bint Zam'a, **Aishah** bint **Abu Bakr**, **Hafsah** bint Umar, Zainab bint Khuzaimah (renamed Umm al-Masakin 'mother of the poor'), Hind bint Abu Umayyah (renamed Umm Salamah), Zainab bint Jahsh (the Prophet's cousin, previously married to his foster-son Zaid), Juwairiyyah bint al-Harith (a defeated Arab chieftain's daughter), Ramlah bint Abu Sufyan (renamed Umm Habibah), Safiyyah bint Huyayy (Jewish), and Maimunah bint al-Harith. Khadijah and Zainab bint Khuzaimah died before the Prophet. Khadijah bore all the Prophet's children except Ibrahim, the son of Maryam the Copt. All were given the title Umm al-Muslimun or 'mother of the faithful' (33:28–34).

Priests servants of shrines who generally fulfil the function of making **sacrifices** and interceding between God and the believers. The role is forbidden in Islam; each person stands before God as an individual, and has no priest (22:37).

Punishment the criminal should always be dealt with fairly and justly according to Islam. Punishment becomes meaningless if it is so soft that it does not affect the offender or satisfy the sense of justice of the wronged person. Yet it must not be unnecessarily cruel or vindictive. The Prophet taught that 'the reward for an injury is an equal injury back; but **forgiveness** is better, and if a person forgives instead, that will earn reward from Allah' (42:40). No person should be above the law, or able to corrupt the law, or feel unprotected by the law. Some Islamic punishments (▶ see **hudud**) are seen as very harsh by the West; they include flogging for public drunkenness and **zinah**, and amputation of the hand for **theft** (5:41; 17:32; 24:2–5). Yet for a true Muslim the real punishment should be to know that Allah is aware of their dishonourable act and they will face it on **Judgement Day**. ▶ See also **diyyah**, **qisas**.

Purdah (*per-daa*) an Urdu word referring to the practice of complete social separation of men and women unless they are members of the same immediate family. This is an extreme version of the requirement that women should never be left alone with men who might take advantage of them. Purdah can be oppressive and an abuse of Islam if it is forced upon women. ▶ See **hijab**.

Q

Qadr ▶ see **al-Qadr**.

Qayamah (*kai-am-aah*) ▶ see **Judgement Day**.

Qiblah (*kib-laah*) the direction of **Makkah**. All Muslims try to face in this direction while praying. **Mosques** usually have a **mihrab** showing the direction; prayer mats sometimes have a compass (and a little booklet with instructions on how to use it); streets and prominent places in Muslim societies often have an arrow to point the direction.

Qisas (*kee-saas*) the idea of exact revenge, or 'an eye for an eye'; this was laid down in the Qur'an in order to *limit* revenge, not to encourage it (42:40). It is always better to forgive and leave the **punishment** to Allah. ▶ See also **Judgement Day**.

Qiyam (*kee-yaam*) the position of standing upright, halfway through the **salah prayer**. ▶ See **rakah**.

Qiyas (*kee-yaas*) from *qasa*, to measure, compare, correlate. This is the principle of working out new rulings or decisions for modern society by comparison with the rules for similar situations in the Qur'an or **hadith**. ▶ See **ijtihad**.

Quraish (*kur-ray-sh*) the leading tribe in and around **Makkah**; the tribe of the Prophet **Muhammad**.

Qur'an (*kur-aan*) the collection of messages Allah revealed to the Prophet **Muhammad** over a period of 23 years (10:57). The word means 'that which is recited'. It is also called the 'Mother of Books' (Umm al-Kitab). A verse is called an **ayah** or 'sign', a chapter is called a **surah** or 'step up'. The complete Qur'an contains 114 surahs, all except one of which begin 'In the name of Allah, the Compassionate, the Merciful'. The surahs are not given in the order the Prophet received them, but the order fixed shortly before he died. The first **revelation** given was the first part of surah 96, and the last was the first part of surah 5. The first surah is now called al-**Fatihah**, 'the opener'. When not in use, the Qur'an should be stored in a respectful manner that keeps it clean and protected; before handling or using it a person should be in a state of **wudu**, and in a suitable frame of mind. While it is being read, people should not chat, eat or drink, make a noise, or behave in a disrespectful manner. It should not be placed on the floor – Muslims often use a wooden stand called a **kursi** or rehl. The handling of Qur'ans in public places such as shops, libraries and schools has upset some Muslims, but what matters is the **niyyah** behind the use of the Holy Book.

Qurban (*kur-baan*) ▶ see **sacrifice**.

R

Rabb (*raab*) the title 'master', used for Allah.

Racism the verbal or physical **persecution** of someone because of their racial origin, colour, accent or physical appearance. Totally forbidden in Islam. (5:9).

Rakah (*rak-aah*) literally, 'bowing'. One complete unit of movements and words during **salah**. It consists of eight separate acts of devotion: **1 takbir** – shutting out the world and its distractions; **2** placing the hands on the chest and praising God, reciting the **Fatihah** and another prayer; **3 ruku** – bowing from the hips to show respect for Allah; **4 qiyam** – straightening up again and acknowledging awareness of God's presence; **5 sujud** or sajda – prostration on the ground, touching the earth with forehead, nose, palms, knees and toes; **6** kneeling up again; **7** sujud repeated; **8** sitting up again and either preparing to repeat the rakah or ending it. At the end of the rakahs, the Muslim performs the salam, turning the head to right and left to greet the **angels**. The number of compulsory rakahs is two for **fajr**, four for **zuhr**, four for **asr**, three for **maghrib** and four for **isha**. Most Muslims perform many more than this set number. It is considered polite to offer two rakahs when entering a **mosque**, as a 'greeting to the mosque'.

The sujud position.

Ramadan (*ram-a-dan*) the month of **fasting**, the ninth month of the Islamic **calendar**.

Rasul (*ra-sool*) a messenger of Allah; a **prophet** who has written a **revelation.** All rasuls were prophets, but not all prophets were rasuls. ▶ See also **nabi**, **nazala**.

Rawdah (*row-daah*) a remembrance feast or service, usually taking place 40 days after the death of a person. It is based on culture, and is a feature of **Shi'ite** communities; generally, however, it is neither compulsory nor normal in Islam.

Record of deeds the work of recording **angels** – two assigned to each person – on which judgement of that person will be based when **Judgement Day** comes (82:10–11). Any good deed remains as a permanent entry, but bad deeds can be obliterated if the offender is genuinely sorry and seeks God's **forgiveness** and also that of the offended party.

Repentance in Arabic, tawbah (*taw-baah*). This means being genuinely sorry for the things we have done wrong, or for not doing the things we ought to have done. When we truly repent, Allah forgives us, even if the persons we have wronged may not be able to do so, but the repentance must be before our death. (2:161; 39:53). ▶ See also **kaffarah**.

Resurrection to rise from the dead. Muslims believe that the whole of humanity will be resurrected at a time when God wills, and face **Judgement Day**. The fact that dead bodies decompose and rot away is no problem, since, for Allah, the renewed creation of a body that has died is no more difficult that the creation of a human's first body; a time will come when each person will be resurrected 'even to the individual fingerprints' (75:1–5). However, our resurrected bodies will probably bear no resemblance to our present ones. Allah said: 'I will create you in forms you know not of' (56:61). ▶ See also **Akhirah**, **al-Ghaib**.

Revelation truths that come from beyond the human mind; messages from God. ▶ See also **nazala**.

Riba (*ree-baa*) interest on loaned money. ▶ See **usury**.

Ruh (*rooh*) the soul. Its exact nature is not known by humans, and many do not believe it exists. However, to a Muslim, the soul is far more important than the body; it is the real person, the abiding essence which persists through all the stages and changes of human life, and endures beyond the **death** of the human body. Theories about souls are many and impossible to prove; for example, that some people can see them; or that they can leave the body while it still lives, and frequently do so during sleep (10:44; 32:16). Muslims believe that, at death, the soul of a good person, although still linked to the body that will face **resurrection** in due course, can range infinite distances and will enjoy its experiences while waiting for **Judgement Day**; the souls of **evil** people, on the other hand, will be earthbound, confined to the **grave**, and suffer torment and despair.

Ruku (*ru-koo*) the bowing position in **salah**. ▶ See **rakah**.

S

Sabians (*sa-bee-ans*) a sect named in the Qur'an, together with **Jews** and **Christians**, as believers in God and the **Judgement Day** who act righteously (2:62). It is thought that they were followers of the **prophet Yahya** (John the Baptist). A community still survives near Basra in southern Iraq.

Sabr (*sab-er*) the attitude of patience or acceptance; not complaining about one's lot in life, but making the best of any situation and seeking to do God's will (3:17).

Sacrifice the killing of an animal while dedicating it to God. This form of slaughter is not to appease, bribe or try to please Allah with an innocent creature's blood (22:37). It is a way of submitting one's meat to God in a dedication which goes on from the moment of killing the animal in a **halal** way to the sharing of food with the poor and needy; and it strengthens the awareness of belonging to the family of all humankind. On the 10th **Dhul-Hijjah** Muslims everywhere sacrifice a sheep, goat, cow or camel, and share a meal in memory of **Ibrahim**'s being prepared to sacrifice **Isma'il**. The feast is known as **Id-ul-Adha**.

Sadaqah (*sad-aa-kaa*) these are acts of voluntary giving or kindness. The Prophet stated that every little act done to please God or to make life more pleasant for others was sadaqah, and brought blessings upon the person who did it. His examples included removing obstacles from people's paths; planting trees and fields to provide food; cheering people up by smiling, speaking comfortingly to them, helping them; reconciling those who are arguing; having a loving and considerate sexual relationship with one's life-partner; giving little presents to people, and so on.

Safavids (*saf-aa-vids*) a **Shi'ite** Muslim dynasty founded by Shah Isma'il, which ruled Persia from 1500 to 1722 CE.

Sahabah (*sa-ha-bah*) a companion, or close friend of the Prophet.

Sahih (*saa-heeh*) the word means 'valid' or 'lawful'. It usually refers to the **hadith** which are truly authentic, with a sound **isnad**. The Sahih al-Bukhari and Sahih Muslim are the two collections of hadith vouched for by the **Sunni** scholars **Imam** Muhammad ibn Isma'il al-*Bukhari* and Abul Husayn *Muslim* ibn al-Hajjaj, and are regarded by all Muslims as reliable.

Saladin or Saleh al-Din ibn Ayyub (1138–93). A military leader of Kurdish origin who became ruler of Egypt and Syria, and defeated the **Crusaders**, led by Richard I ('the Lionheart'), in Palestine. His dynasty, known as the Ayyubids, ruled in Syria from 1169 to 1260.

Salah (*saa-laah*) the ritual compulsory **prayer** (▶ see **five pillars of Islam**), performed five times per day (20:130) under special conditions in the manner taught by the Prophet in the Arabic language. ▶ See also **rakah**.

Clocks showing the times for prayer at the mosque (start on the right!). The times change with the sunrise and sunset.

Salat-ul-janaza (*saa-lat-ul-jan-a-zaa*) the funeral **prayer** said for a dead person. It consists of two **rakahs**, but there is no bowing to earth.

Salat-ul-Jumu'ah (*saa-lat-ul-joo-maah*) the 'Friday prayer' – the one occasion during the week when all male Muslims are urged to try to come together in the **mosque** to pray. It takes the place of the **zuhr** prayer, and consists of the double **khutbah** and two **rakahs**. (62:9).

Sawm ▶ see **fasting**.

Sa'y (*sa-ee*) often spelt sai, this is the second ritual of **hajj**. After circling the **Ka'bah** and praying, pilgrims walk briskly between the small hills of Safa and Marwah, now an enclosed passageway. (Disabled people have a wheelchair path down the middle.) The walk commemorates the desperate search of **Hajar** for water, and symbolises the **soul**'s search for that which gives true spiritual life.

School ▶ see **madrassah**.

Sermon ▶ see **khutbah**.

Sermon, the Last the speech given by the Prophet on the occasion of the **hajj** in 632 CE, to a crowd of some 140,000 people. That speech may be summarised as follows: 'O people, listen to my words carefully, for I do not know whether I will meet you again on such an occasion as this. You must live at peace with one another. Everyone must respect the rights and properties of their neighbours. There must be no rivalry or enmity among you. Just as you regard this month as sacred, so regard the life and property of every Muslim in the same way. Remember, you will surely appear before God to answer for your actions. All believers are the same family . . . you are not allowed to take things from another Muslim unless it is given to you willingly. You are to look after your families with all your heart, and be kind to the women God has entrusted to you . . . O People, reflect on my words . . . I leave behind me two things, the Qur'an and the **sunnah**. If you follow these you will not fail. Listen to me very carefully. Worship God, be steadfast in **prayer**,' **fast** during **Ramadan**, pay **zakah** to the less fortunate. People, no **prophet** or messenger will come after me, and no new faith will emerge. All those who listen to me will pass on my words to others, and those to others again.'

Seveners a **Shi'ite** sect that believes the seventh **imam** disappeared mysteriously and will reappear at the end of time, and that meanwhile he guides the faithful mystically. ▶ See **Isma'ilis**, **Twelvers**.

Sex in Islam, sex is considered as one of God's gifts to humanity; it is not sinful or dirty or degrading, unless it is abused. Its purposes include encouraging deep love and affection between husband and wife, teaching compassion, co-operation and **generosity**, and giving in a small way a glimpse of the wonderful joys of **Paradise**. Living without sex (▶ see **monasticism**) is disapproved of in Islam. The sort of sex that brings **sadaqah** is that which is skilled, modest and generous, seeking happiness in putting one's partner before oneself.

Sex outside marriage ▶ see **zinah**.

Shahadah (*shaa-had-aah*) literally, 'witnessing', this is the first of the **five pillars of Islam**. It is a declaration of faith that God really does exist, and that **Muhammad** really was a true **prophet**. The words in Arabic are, 'Ash-hadu an la ilaha il-allahu wa Muhammad ar-rasulullah' ('I believe – or I bear witness – that there is no God but Allah and that Muhammad is His Prophet').

Shahid (*shaa-heed*) a person who 'bears witness' to God by giving up his or her own life; a martyr who dies for the faith. (2:154; 3:169–71; 22:58–9).

Shaikh (*sha-ik*) a Sufi (▶ see **Sufism**) master or teacher such as Shaikh Nazim, the leader of the Naqshbandi Sufis; the name (spelt 'Sheikh') also refers to a tribal leader.

Shari'ah (*shaa-ree-yaa*) from *shari*, a road, and *shara'a*, to begin, enter, introduce, prescribe. The Way of Islam, or Islamic law based on the Qur'an and **sunnah** ('This is My straight path, so follow it, and do not follow paths which will separate you from this path' – 6:153; 57:28), this is the code of behaviour for a Muslim, which determines whether any action or detail of life is **halal** or **haram**. It involves transforming faith in God into action, faith being meaningless without the deeds that express it in action. ▶ See also **amal**, **iman**.

Shaytan (*shai-taan*) literally, 'rebellious', 'proud' – the Muslim name for the Devil, who is also called Iblis. The Qur'an states that he was the chief of the **jinn**, and that he used his **free will** to refuse to bow down to the first human when God requested him to. One might think this showed piety, not wishing to bow down to any other but Allah, but what it did in fact reveal was pride and disobedience; he questioned God's will, and thought he knew better! Since the confrontation over **Adam**, Shaytan has never ceased deceiving and misleading people, and trying to lure them away from Allah. (2:34–6; 3:36; 4:117–20; 5:94; 7:11–18, 200–201; 8:48; 14:22; 15:17, 31–4; 16:98–100; 17:61–5; 18:50; 20:116–23; 22:53–4; 24:21; 35:6; 36:60; 38:71–85).

Shi'ah (*shee-aah*) literally, 'followers', the word usually refers to the Shi'at Ali, or followers of **Ali**, the **Shi'ites**.

Shi'ite (*shee-ites*) originally, they were supporters of the Prophet's son-in-law **Ali**, and claimed that he had really been the intended first caliph. Sunnis, on the other hand, accept the succession of **Abu Bakr** followed by **Umar** and **Uthman**. Ali finally became the fourth caliph, although Shi'ites still regard him as the first. After Ali's death, his son Hassan contested the **Ummayyad** chief **Mu'awiyah**'s claim to the caliphate, as Hassan's brother **Hussein** continued to do when Hassan died. The Shi'ites went on choosing their leaders from the Prophet's family for the next ten generations. While the quality of the caliphs inevitably varied, the **Sunni** view tended to be that peace under a less than perfect ruler was better than anarchy. Shi'ites, however, maintained that the ruler should be the ultimate spiritual authority, and descended from the Prophet – hence their series of special **imams** (▶ see **Ayatollah**, **Seveners**, **Twelvers**). Several Shi'ite practices are not accepted by Sunni Muslims, e.g. **mutah**, **rawdahs**, and the veneration of saints, imams and the Prophet's descendants. Shi'ite demonstrations of religious fervour, for example at **Ashurah**, are often seen by those who do not share their feelings as appealing to dangerous emotions. In fact, only about 10 per cent of Muslims are Shi'ite; the rest are Sunni.

Shirk (*sheerk*) literally, 'association', this is the concept that the unity of God is divisible; that God is not supreme or alone; or the belief that some other entity shares God's power and has the right to judge, or forgive sins, or make permissible what is forbidden, or forbid what is permissible; or the belief that the spiritual God can have sons or daughters. To make an **idol** out of any admired hero, or cult, sect, commitment or hobby is also a form of shirk. (2:116; 6:22–4, 100–101, 133–7, 163; 10:68; 24:35).

Shurah (*shoo-raah*) the duty of Islamic leaders, no matter how high-powered they may be, to consult properly with those they represent, in order to give guidance that is acceptable and reasonable to those who have to follow it.

Sirah (*see-raah*) a written 'life' or biography of the Prophet **Muhammad**. The earliest were those of Zuhri and of Ibn Ishaq, Zuhri's disciple.

Slander to speak ill of another, usually behind their back. The Prophet felt that if you couldn't speak well of someone, it was better not to speak at all; he described **backbiting** as 'eating the flesh' of the person talked about. (24:19; 49:12).

Slaughter **halal** slaughter has to be done in a particular way, the aim being to kill the **animal** in the most humane way possible. The animal should not be in any state of neglect, fear or discomfort beforehand; it should be held as gently and firmly as possible while being slaughtered, and have its throat cut across the jugular vein with a very sharp knife. A prayer dedicating the animal to Allah should be uttered. The blood should then be allowed to drain out swiftly. To kill an animal cruelly is a gross abuse of Islam, and any animal made to suffer cannot be halal to eat, even if the other halal rules were followed when it was killed.

Slaves slavery was not forbidden in Islam at the time of the Prophet – it was considered acceptable as a way for people to pay off their debts. However, a good Muslim would always choose to forgive a person their debts rather than see them in slavery. The Prophet and the **sahabah** set free many slaves; and Islam granted many rights to slaves, such as the right to earn and save money, and the right not to be abused or forced into sex with their masters or their relatives. Many Muslim **converts** were slaves or ex-slaves.

Soul ▶ see **ruh**.

Stoning the Devil ▶ see **Ibrahim**, **Isma'il**, **Jamarat**, **Mina**.

Subhah (*sub-aah*) a string of beads representing the names of God revealed in the Qur'an. (You will find these names listed on pages 79 to 80.) Many Muslims praise God after the daily **prayers**, using the beads as an 'aid'. They say 'subhan-Allah' ('glory be to God'), 'Al-hamdu-li-Llah' ('thanks be to God') and '**Allahu Akbar**' ('God is the most great') 33 times each as they pass the beads. A different bead divides each set of 33. Some people say the same prayer using the finger joints of their right hand to count.

A 99-bead subhah. Sometimes they only have 33 beads.

Successor ► see **caliph**.

Sufism (*soo-fism*) in Arabic, **tasawwuf**, probably derived from *safa* ('purity') or *suf* ('wool', the material of the modest garments of the Prophet and his **sahabah**). Sufism is often called Islamic mysticism. It emphasises the need for personal purification and piety through constant awareness and love of God, and honest and humble self-knowledge. Sufis often choose a way of life based on self-denial and meditation, sometimes making use of such ritual practices as the sacred dance, or the chanting of the name of Allah (► see **dhikr**). Muslims differ greatly in their attitudes towards Sufism; some regard it as the real

heart of the faith – keeping true Islam alive in times of corruption and loss of spirituality; others see it as dangerously emotional, and removed from the practical discipline of the Islamic way of life. The main Sufi groups in the UK are the Naqshbandi and Murabitun. ► See **Shaikh**.

Suhur a light breakfast taken before dawn when one is about to commence a day's **fasting**.

Suicide deliberately putting an end to one's own life. This is just as **haram** in Islam as the taking of any other person's life, and is regarded as a great sin. The person who commits suicide is usually trying to escape what seem at the time unbearable pressures of life; but Muslims believe that one continues to 'live' in the next state of existence (► see **Akhirah**), and may then experience the added pain and guilt of the suffering one has caused those left behind. Fortunately, the mercy of God is such that it takes into consideration the state of mind of the suicide. No blame is attached to the person whose mind was disturbed, or who is no longer capable of rational thought. And, after all, how can we presume to know the extent of Allah's mercy? The kindest thing a bereaved Muslim can do is to pray for the **soul** of the person who committed suicide, and themselves forgive them, so that the soul can at least be at peace from that aspect of the pain.

Sujud (*su-jood*) this means bowing to earth in humility, Muslims touching the ground with the five points of the body: forehead, nose, hands, knees and toes. ▶ See also **rakah, salah.**

Suleiman (*sul-ee-maan*) a son of **Dawud** the **prophet**, King of the **Jews**. Suleiman (Solomon) reigned after him. He was famous for his great **hikmah** (wisdom). The Qur'an records several aspects of his life, notably his conquests, his love of horses, his conversion of the Queen of Sheba, and his ability to communicate with animals and birds. (2:102; 6:84; 21:79–82; 27:15–44; 34:12–14; 38:30–40).

Summayah (*soo-mai-yaah*) the first Muslim martyr. She is said to have been the seventh **convert** to Islam, and the **Quraish** tortured her by dressing her in metal armour, tying her up in the blazing sun and then stabbing her to death. ▶ See **shahid.**

Sunnah (*soon-naah*) from *sanna* – to shape, form, establish – it is the Prophet's example or way of life, everything he said, did, approved of or condemned. Sunnah actions are not compulsory: those who followed the Prophet's sunnah would be rewarded for it, but there was no **punishment** or blame for those who did not. The real importance of following the sunnah lies not in unimportant details, but in following the Prophet's general path of compassion, gentleness, honesty, courage and truth. (33:21).

Sunni mainstream Islam; Muslims who follow the **sunnah** of the Prophet. They also accept the first three **caliphs** and place **Ali** fourth. ▶ See also **Shi'ah, Shi'ite.**

Surah (*su-raah*) a chapter of the Qur'an. The word means 'a step up'.

Superstition a form of **kufr**, or lack of belief or **trust** in God. No object, charm or incantation can possibly overrule the will of Allah (7:188; 35:2). Charms (*ruqya* in Arabic) – such things as horse-shoes, hare's feet, and so on – are forbidden in Islam; even a pious charm like a miniature Qur'an or little bits of Qur'an text kept in a locket are disapproved of, for they encourage people to think they have power in themselves. ▶ See also **divination, magic.**

SWT this stands for 'Subhanahu wa Ta'ala' (*sub-han-aa-hu waa ta-aa-laa*) – 'May He be praised and His lordship of **creation** affirmed' – words frequently added after the name of Allah has been used. ▶ See also **pbuh.**

Taharah (*ta-ha-raah*) ▶ see **cleanliness**.

Taif (*ta-if*) a mountain oasis-town in Saudi Arabia, where the Prophet was rejected before his **Hijrah** to **Madinah**.

Tajwid (*taj-weed*) the art of correct pronunciation when reciting the Qur'an.

Takbir (*tak-beer*) the utterance of the phrase '**Allahu Akbar**' ('Allah is the most great').

Takfir (*tak-feer*) this is the practice of accusing others of being **kafir**. It is a symptom of **extremism** which shows a lack of **tolerance** for differences of opinion and expression. For example, extremists frequently describe **Christians** and **Jews** as kafirun (nonbelievers), even though the Qur'an calls them the '**People of the Book**' and recognises that they have received **revelation** and believe in the one true God (29:46). The Prophet himself regarded all non-Muslims as potential Muslims, to be welcomed.

Talaq (*ta-laaq*) the formal procedure of a husband stating that he wishes to **divorce** his wife. The **iddah** then begins. The husband has to officially pronounce 'I divorce you' three times, once at the end of each of three consecutive months, during which time the husband and wife must continue to live in the same house but without resuming a sexual relationship. Family and friends do their best to reconcile them; if they resume a sexual relationship, the divorce is instantly cancelled. At the end of the three months the divorce is absolute, and both may remarry. The Prophet made it very clear that to pronounce 'I divorce you' three times on one occasion only counted as *one* occasion, so where Muslim men have claimed to be divorced after doing so, they are abusing Islam.

Taqwa (*tak-waa*) consciousness of God, the realisation that God always sees you, even if you cannot see God. A person who has this awareness is called *muttaqeen*. It brings with it a deep sense of closeness, serenity, personal responsibility. (3:134–46; 8:2; 21:49; 23:57–61).

Tarawih (*ta-ra-weeh*) or salat-al-tarawih, 'prayer of pauses'. These are extra **prayers** made voluntarily during the nights of the month of **Ramadan**. Each evening Muslims meet at the **mosque** for a service that may be as long as 40 **rakahs** with a pause after every 4; during this month the Qur'an is recited in sections, the aim being to get through the whole **revelation**. The **sunnah** of the Prophet was actually either 8 rakahs or 20, according to which tradition one follows.

Tariqah (*taar-ee kaa*) a way or path, whereby the teachings of Islam may be applied to the realm of inner experience. The word is used by Sufis to mean the 'science of the soul' – the inner aspect of **Shari'ah**. In **Sufism**, it is the combination of Tariqah and Shari'ah that leads to **haqiqah** (truth), i.e. knowledge of God.

Tarji (*taar-jee*) the practice of repeating **adhan** to oneself in a low voice just before commencing **salah**.

Tasawwuf (*ta-sa-woof*) the word for spiritual insight. ▶ See **Sufism**.

Tasbih (*tas-beeh*) another word for **subhah**.

Tashahhud (*tash-aa-hood*) literally, 'to make **shahadah**'. In the context of **prayer** it is a formula which includes the shahadah, said in the final sitting position of each two-**rakah** cycle. It often includes a blessing on the holy Prophet **Muhammad**.

Tawaf (*ta-waaf*) the first act of pilgrims when arriving at the **Ka'bah** on **hajj**, no matter what hour of day or night. Pilgrims circle the central shrine in an anti-clockwise procession seven times, running the first three circuits if they can. This is called the tawaf al-ifadah (*ta-waaf al-if-aa-daah*). Disabled and old people may be carried on special stretcher-chairs. They use the **Black Stone** to count their circuits, raising their hands in salute each time they pass. Many, if they are able to get to it, touch it or kiss it in their fervour – but this must not be mistaken for worship. It is not an **idol**. When the pilgrims return to the Ka'bah after the **wuquf**, they perform another circling, the tawaf al-qadun (*ta-waaf al-ka-doon*). If they circle yet again before going home, it is called tawaf al-wida (*ta-waaf al-wee-daah*) – the farewell tawaf.

Tawakkul (*ta-wak-kool*) ▶ see **trust**.

Tawarruh (*ta-waar-ooh*) the sitting position for **tashahhud** – the right foot upright with the toes on the ground, pointing towards **Makkah**.

Tawbah (*taw-baah*) ▶ see **repentance**.

Tawhid (*taw-heed*) literally, 'one', 'alone'. The doctrine of the one-ness of God. Nothing is remotely like God and nothing can be compared to Him (our knowledge and capacity for imagination being in any case far too limited) – see surah 6:103; 112. To call God 'He' is only a custom; God has no human gender. Allah is totally 'other' than His **creation**, transcendent – which means outside time, eternal, and only known as He chooses to reveal Himself (6:103).

God is the Alone, the Almighty, the Supreme; He is the **First Cause**, Creator and Sustainer, Judge and Decider of our fates. He is also at the same time immanent – which means He is so close to us and intimately involved with us that He is aware of our every thought; He is closer to us than our jugular veins. (50:16; 2:186). ▶ See also **kufr**, **shirk**, **takfir**.

Tawrah (*taw-raah*) the Muslim name for the Torah, or revelation given to the **prophet Musa**. Muslims regard the collection of Musaic writings contained in the Old Testament as a different thing, however. They maintain that although those writings originated with Musa, they have been styled and put together by later human editors, and are not the revelations just as Musa received them. (11:110; 53:36; 87:19).

Tayammum (*tay-am-mum*) ritual washing using sand, dust or earth when no water is available for **wudu** or **ghusl** (4:43).

Temporary marriage ▶ see **mutah**.

Tests human beings have to cope with all sorts of circumstances during their lifetimes; some involve great suffering and distress, some involve challenges such as luxury and power. The Muslim regards every circumstance as a test to prove how much a person is able to respond and act according to God's will in any given situation. Islam

promises that no one shall be faced with a burden that is too much for them to bear. (2:155–6, 286; 3:139–42; 23:62).

Theft in Arabic, sariqah (*saa-ree-kaah*) – stealing something from another person. This is so serious a sin in Islam that it is considered as a denial of the faith. Those who steal cannot truly believe that Allah sees them and that they will be called to account for their deed on **Judgement Day**. Theft can be given a hadd punishment (▶ see **hudud**), the cutting off of a hand (5:41). However, to receive such a sentence the thief must be a Muslim, and be adult and sane; also, not forced to steal, nor driven to it by hunger. If the thief later repents, he or she can be forgiven and can re-enter Islam. It is worth noting that for a Muslim the real deterrent should be the shame of loss of Islam.

Tilawah (*til-aa-waa*) reading the Qur'an with purpose and concentration.

Time-span the amount of time one is granted to live on earth as a human being. Muslims regard their lives here as a gift, which they must be ready to return whenever Allah wills. (3:145; 16:61; 53:42–7).

Tolerance being prepared to listen to and consider the opinions of other people. Islam asks for tolerance towards all people, whether they be Muslims or non-Muslims; the Prophet said that no one could call himself a Muslim whose neighbour felt threatened by harm at his hands. A Muslim is required to show by example the way of life pleasing to Allah, and to warn – not enforce, dominate or despise (88:21–2). Even when confronted by **evil** in a person, one should continue to love the person, while hating the evil that has spoiled them.

Trust in Arabic, tawakkul (*ta-wak-kool*) – confidence that Allah sees everything and, no matter what the circumstances of life, things will work out for good if we trust God and have patience (▶ see **sabr**). It does not imply passive acceptance when things go wrong, but rather having faith that Allah moves in mysterious ways unknown to us to bring about His will. ▶ See also **istikhara**.

Twelvers also called Ithna Ashari and Ja'fari, this is the mainstream

Shi'ite school of thought based on the rulings of the 12 Shi'ite **imams** (**Ali** being the first, followed by the Prophet's grandsons). The 12th imam mysteriously disappeared. However, Twelvers do not regard him as dead but still alive. He is known as the **Hidden Imam**. ▶ See **Mahdi**.

Tyranny in Arabic, tughyan (*toog-yaan*) – unkind oppression and fanaticism. The Prophet stated that to knowingly support an oppressor was to depart from Islam, and that the most excellent **jihad** was to speak the truth in the face of a tyrannical ruler. Some of the worst tyrants rule nothing more than their own family: they may be husbands, wives or even spoiled children or overdomineering parents. Tughyan can also apply to the sin of arrogance – 'religious' or otherwise – which makes others feel small or uncomfortable or stupid.

U

Uhud (*oo-hood*) the site of the second battle of Muslims against Makkans, in 625 (▶ see **Badr**), when the Muslims were defeated. The Prophet himself was wounded and lost two teeth. He used the defeat to

teach that he was not 'superhuman'; they should not have acted so hastily and relied on their fallible human judgement. Success only came by waiting obediently for Allah's directions. (3:152).

Ulama (*oo-la-maa*) plural of *alim*; scholars of Islamic law and jurisprudence.

Umar (*oo-maar*) second **caliph** (634–44). Famous for his fiery temper, Umar ibn al-Khattab was originally a fierce enemy of Islam, determined to defend the **idols** of **Makkah** and slay the Prophet. When he discovered that his sister Fatimah and her husband had been converted, he rushed to their house, intending to kill her; but on hearing a **surah** being recited which seemed to speak to him personally, he became a **convert** himself. He came to be one of the Prophet's closest and most devoted companions, and when his daughter **Hafsah**'s husband was killed the Prophet married her, and so he became the Prophet's father-in-law. During his caliphate the Muslims captured Syria and Palestine, and he went to **Jerusalem** himself and began the repairs at the site of the Jewish temple with his own hands. He granted a decree of **tolerance** to the **Christian** community there. He was loved for his humility, **generosity** and fairness in spite of a reputation for sternness. His death was at the hands of a man against whose case he had judged; the assassin stabbed him while he was praying at the dawn **prayer**. Before he died, he appointed a six-man committee to elect his successor.

Ummah (*umm-aah*) literally, 'community', this is the 'family' of Islam, the community of believers.

Muslims from an immense diversity of cultures and languages all live by the same faith, following the same **sunnah**. (2:143; 3:103, 110; 9:71; 49:10).

Umm al-Kitab (*umm al-kit-aab*) the Qur'an, the 'Mother of Books'.

Ummayyads (*umm-eye-ads*) a leading tribe amongst the **Quraish**. The third **caliph**, **Uthman**, was an Ummayyad, and after his cousin **Mu'awiyah** became the fifth caliph, the office remained with that family until the time of the Abbasid rising (661–750). The collapse of the Ummayyad dynasty was due largely to their increase in **wealth** and power, which brought about a corresponding decrease in spirituality. Muslims wished to bring back the original purity of the Prophet's teaching.

Umrah (*um-raah*) the 'Lesser Pilgrimage' – a **pilgrimage** to **Makkah**, and all the ritual connected with that event, made at any time other than the 8th–13th **Dhul-Hijjah**.

Unfurling the **hajj** events that take place after the **wuquf** at **Mount Arafat**. They include the stoning of the **jamarat** at **Mina**, the Feast of **Sacrifice** (**Id-ul-Adha**), the shaving of men's heads and cutting of women's hair, the return to normal clothing and ending of the state of **ihram**, a return to the **Ka'bah**, and a visit to **Madinah** and other historic Muslim sites.

Unity the ideal for Muslims is that they should all form one **ummah**. The Prophet likened the community of Islam to one body; when a part of it was hurt, the other parts ached. The divisive Muslim was in danger of departing from Islam through religious pride and intolerance (▶ see **extremism, organisations**). Every Muslim should regard every other Muslim as a brother or sister, in a worldwide network of those who submit to Allah's will. ▶ See also **Sermon, the Last**.

Usury in Arabic, **riba** – literally, exploitation, taking advantage. Muslims are allowed to make money in fair trade, but not from exploitation (2:274–5; 3:130; 4:161). Those who possess **wealth** are asked to help the poor by lending them what they need without interest. ('If the debtor is in difficulty, grant him time until it is easy for him to repay … your repayment [from Allah] would be greater if you cancelled the debt altogether', 2:280.) The Prophet also forbade needy Muslims from trying to *borrow* except in cases of dire necessity (e.g. life-threatening lack of food, clothing or medical treatment); even then, the borrowing should be limited to no more than the exact amount needed and should be repaid, by whatever reasonable means possible, as quickly as possible.

Uthman (*uth-maan*) third **caliph** of Islam (644–56). A rich, handsome and idealistic youth of the **Ummayyad** family of the **Quraish**, he donated all his **wealth** to the cause of Islam. He married two of the Prophet's daughters – first Ruqaiyyah, and then, after she died, Umm Kulthum. He was gentle and kind-hearted, and became caliph when he was an old man. His administration lacked the discipline of **Umar**, and he was accused of appointing too many friends and relatives to key positions, even though he would have argued that they merited these posts. When he was 80, he was asked to abdicate, but he refused. His cousin, the ruler of Egypt, had imposed harsh taxes and Uthman had not intervened; a group of Egyptians assassinated him whilst he was at prayer. His cousin **Mu'awiyah**, Governor of Syria, became the fifth caliph.

Values qualities most valued by Muslims are devotion to Allah; honesty, compassion, kindness, **generosity**, courage, patience, justice, **tolerance**, **forgiveness**, sincerity, truth, modesty, chastity, fortitude, and responsibility.

Veiled women ▶ see **hijab**, **purdah**.

Visions the gift of 'seeing' something through the 'mind's eye', because God has wished to raise the awareness of the person receiving the vision above the limits of their physical surroundings. For example, people have had visions of spiritual beings (e.g. **angels**) not normally visible to humans; or places beyond our normal human limitations (e.g. the Prophet's journey from **Jerusalem** through the heavens); or of events which will take place in the future (e.g. the **prophet Isa** prophesying the coming of a Son of Man, or Comforter – Muslims believe that to be a prophecy of the coming of **Muhammad**); or of details beyond human knowledge (e.g. the Prophet's grandfather **Abd al-Muttalib** being shown the **Zamzam** spring, which had been lost to knowledge). The experience of seeing visions is not limited to Islam, of course, but is recorded for every religion, often having the effect of changing or influencing the recipient's entire future life.

Vivisection experimentation with living creatures. In Islam, anything which inflicts suffering or cruelty is **haram**; anything which promotes the common or individual good is **halal**. Vivisection in experiments for purposes of developing luxury goods such as make-up is clearly a haram practice. However, when it is for medical research, which could be for the good of humanity, the case is very much more debatable.

Wahhabism (*waa-hab-ism*) a 'purist' reform movement founded by Muhammad ibn Abd al-Wahhab (1703–92). It was criticised for its lack of **tolerance** and for concentrating on the rigid observance of ritual duties as opposed to spirituality.

Wahy (*waa-hee*) insight, the ability to understand **revelation** and the inner meaning of messages from God.

Wajib (*waa-jib*) ▶ see **fard**.

Wali (*waa-lee*) a person who is particularly saintly and compassionate. The term is also used for a guardian – a person who has responsibility for another, or a trusted representative. ▶ See **nikah**.

Walimah (*waa-lee-maah*) a party, feast, or celebration, given by the husband's side of the family after a wedding. Its purpose is to publicise the fact that the couple are married and about to live together. ▶ See also **marriage, nikah**.

Waqf (*wak-f*) the donation of certain sources of income (e.g. land or property revenue) to the service of a religious community such as a **mosque**, college, **school** or hospital, to provide for its upkeep and running costs.

Waraqa ibn Nawfal (*war-a-kaa ib-n naw-fal*) the cousin of the Prophet's first wife **Khadijah**. He was a **hanif Christian**, and tradition suggests he had translated a **Gospel** into Arabic. He had concluded from his studies that both **Musa** and **Isa** had foretold the coming of another **prophet** (see Bible, Deuteronomy 18:18 and the Gospel of St John 16:13–15). It was to Waraqa, then 100 years old and blind, that Khadijah turned for advice concerning the Prophet's experience on the **Night of Power**. Waraqa was overjoyed to have lived to see the new messenger of God, but also warned the Prophet that he would face persecution and be rejected by his own people.

Wealth the Prophet stated that 'wealth does not lie in the abundance of worldly goods, but true richness is the richness of the **soul**'. He also taught that the real **test** of his **ummah** would be wealth. Did he perhaps foresee the time when many Muslim nations would have great riches from oil revenues? (64:15).

Wedding ▶ see **nikah**.

Witr (*wit-r*) the praying of an extra **rakah** to make the total come to an odd number – a preference of the Prophet.

Women as regards value and spirituality, there is no difference between male and female in Islam

(33:35). ('All people are equal, as the teeth of a comb' – **hadith**.) As regards talent and ability, it is the duty of Muslims of both sexes to study and improve themselves so far as is possible, and to be as useful to the community as possible. As regards the biological nature of the sexes, Islam recognises that women have certain extra burdens such as menstruation and childbearing, and therefore demands that men should be alert to their problems, sympathetic in their dealings with women (especially in the home and the workplace), appreciative of women's sacrifices, and supportive with their greater strength and ability to earn income and provide home bases. In return, men have the right to expect loyalty, support and (hopefully) love. (4:34).

Work it is a Muslim's duty to work to earn a living, and the Prophet regarded the very humblest of tasks as dignified and honourable. However, certain kinds of work are **haram** for Muslims, for example anything that degrades or exploits, or is dishonest, immoral or abusive. Muslims should not take to **begging**, unless they have no other choice.

Wudu (*wu-thoo*) often spelt wuzu, the ritual wash before **prayer** or

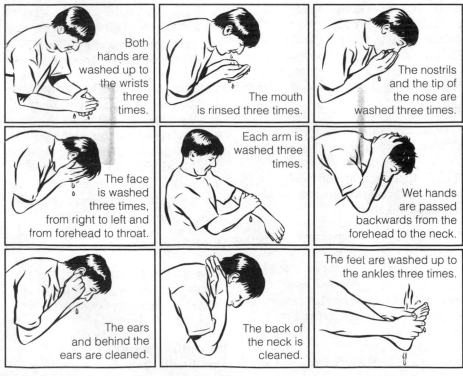

Both hands are washed up to the wrists three times.

The mouth is rinsed three times.

The nostrils and the tip of the nose are washed three times.

The face is washed three times, from right to left and from forehead to throat.

Each arm is washed three times.

Wet hands are passed backwards from the forehead to the neck.

The ears and behind the ears are cleaned.

The back of the neck is cleaned.

The feet are washed up to the ankles three times.

The wudu or ritual wash.

reading of the Qur'an. The wash follows a set pattern: the declaration of **intention** to turn to God; washing the hands up to the wrists three times; rinsing the mouth three times; snuffing water into the nostrils three times; washing the face three times; washing the arms up to the elbows three times; passing wet hands over the top of the head and round the back of the neck; wiping out the ears with the index finger, and the back of the neck with the thumbs; washing the feet to the ankles three times (5:7). This wash will do for more than one prayer provided that the state of wudu is not broken by anything unclean leaving the body, or by unconsciousness. ▶ See also **tayammum**.

Wuquf (*wu-koof*) this is the stand before God at **Mount Arafat**, 24 kilometres east of **Makkah**, on the 9th **Dhul-Hijjah**. The stand takes place between noon and dusk, and without it a pilgrim's **hajj** is invalid, and becomes an **umrah**. It commences with the **zuhr prayer**, and ends with the **asr**, a time of

great spiritual power, when around two million pilgrims bow down together before God in silence. It commemorates the **forgiveness** and reunion of **Adam** and Hawwah, and their release from sin. The sins of pilgrims are 'washed away' and they renew their allegiance to Allah and become 'new'.

The stand at Mount Arafat.

Yahya (*yaah-yaa*) John the Baptist, the cousin of the **prophet Isa** and a prophet himself, miraculously born to the Jewish priest Zakariyah (3:38–41; 6:85; 19:2–15; 21:89–90). His followers were known as **Sabians**, 'dippers' or 'dyers', from his practice of baptism in the River Jordan. Once 'dipped', the 'fabric' of the **convert** was completely 'dyed', or changed to the new way of Islam, or submission to Allah.

Yathrib (*yath-rib*) ▶ see **Madinah**.

Yunus (*yoo-noos*) also called Zun-nun (*zu-noon*) – 'companion of the fish'. He was sent to preach **repentance** to the Assyrians, and was swallowed up by a huge sea-creature – punishment for his annoyance when they did not repent. He prayed to Allah for **forgiveness** and was restored. (4:163; 6:86; 10:98; 21:87; 37:139–48; 68:48–50).

Yusuf (*yoo-soof*) the Muslim name for the **prophet** Joseph, the son of Yaqub (Jacob). Sold by his brothers as a slave, he rose to prominence in Egypt through his gift of interpreting dreams. The Qur'an gives the story of Yusuf being sold to the Aziz ('the Exalted in Rank', known as Potiphar in the Bible), probably the Pharaoh's chief eunuch, whose unhappy wife Zulaikha attempted to seduce Yusuf. The full story of Yusuf and his imprisonment in Egypt, and the coming of his brothers to Egypt, is given in surah 12.

Zabur (*zab-oor*) the **revelation** granted to **Dawud**. It is not identical to the Book of Psalms presented in the Old Testament. (4:163).

Zahid (*zaa-heed*) an ascetic. ▶ See **zuhd**.

Zaid ibn Haritha (*zay-id ib-n har-ee-thaa*) the foster-son of the Prophet, a slave-boy given to him by **Khadijah** on their wedding day. When the boy's family traced him and offered to ransom him, he begged to stay with the Prophet, and was granted his freedom. He married the Prophet's nurse Umm Aieman (by whom he had a son Usamah), and later the Prophet's cousin Zainab, but that marriage failed.

Zaid ibn Thabit (*zay-id ib-un tha-bit*) a man the Prophet relied upon as his secretary. He was given the task of writing down all the separate **revelations** of the Qur'an and compiling them into one book. He was himself a **hafiz**, and the text he put together contained no editorial comment; nothing was added and nothing removed. The order of the verses was ordained by God, and checked by the **angel Jibril** before the Prophet died. When the volume was completed, it was kept in the care of **Umar**'s daughter **Hafsah**, and copies of this text were sent to the chief Muslim centres by **Caliph Uthman**.

Zakah (*zak-aah*) this is the compulsory payment of money or possessions to help the poor, the needy, the sick, the imprisoned, or Muslim mission workers, and which therefore 'cleanses' a Muslim's **wealth**. It comes from the word *zakiya*, meaning 'to be pure', 'to cleanse'. If in the form of money (cash, bank savings and jewellery), the amount of zakah given should be 2.5 per cent of savings (the surplus of a person's income once their own and their family's needs have been taken care of and a level known as **nisab** has been reached). Other examples of zakah are 20 per cent of any mining produce; 10 per cent of

the harvest from rain-watered land; 5 per cent from irrigated land; one cow per 30; one sheep or goat per 40; one sheep or goat per five camels. Zakah is one of the **five pillars of Islam**, a regular annual duty and not merely charity given out of kindness, which is called **sadaqah** (2:195, 210, 264, 270; 9:60). Its purpose is to limit the amount of money withdrawn from circulation in society. If money is just 'saved' by an individual, it is not being used and nobody gets the benefit of it.

Zakat-ul-Fitr (*zak-at-ul-fit-er*) a special donation to charity made during or at the end of **Ramadan**, to enable poor Muslims to celebrate **Id-ul-Fitr**.

Zamzam (*zamzam*) the spring of water shown by the **angel Jibril** to **Hajar**, which saved her son **Isma'il**. The **Ka'bah** was built beside it. It was covered up by the predecessors of the **Quraish** and its location was only rediscovered as the result of a **vision** granted to the Prophet's grandfather **Abd al-Muttalib**. Thereafter, his clan (the Hashimites) looked after the spring and enjoyed the privilege of offering water to pilgrims. Muslims on **hajj** usually drink from the spring (this is not compulsory), and take water as souvenirs; some dip their white **ihram** cloths in it and keep them to act as their shrouds when they die (▶ see **burial**).

Zealotry zeal generally means enthusiasm; zealotry in religion is expressed when the desire to please God becomes excessive, going beyond the bounds of what is required, from motives of religious pride or unhealthy extremes of humility. Genuine as it may be, if the desire to please God is expressed too publicly it can become an embarrassment and irritant to others, and drive them away. (5:90). ▶ See **extremism**.

Zinah (*zin-aah*) sex outside **marriage**. Islam requires all sexual activity to be within the bounds of a married relationship, and condemns **sex** before marriage (fornication), and sex with any person outside the marriage (adultery; 17:32), or with any person of the same sex (▶ see **homosexuality**). If a marriage is not successful, sex outside the partnership is still not excusable until a **divorce** has been granted. Part of the agreement of marriage is that husband and wife should always do their best to satisfy their partner, and not deny them sexual satisfaction, so long as they are not ill or in pain. If one partner refuses to have sexual relations with the other for longer than four months without mutual agreement, it may be grounds for divorce. In pre-Muslim Middle-Eastern societies adultery was frequently punished by death, and the **hadith** record that even the Prophet allowed the death penalty for it on occasions. The penalty actually laid down in the Qur'an was a flogging. Adulterers were also refused permission to

marry non-adulterers – having shown that they could not be trusted (24:2–3). The **madhhabs** disagree on whether the punishment for a married person committing zinah should be flogging, exile or death, though this is rarely inflicted as it requires four male witnesses to the act itself, each capable of identifying the two parties with certainty – stoning someone without this evidence would count as murder. If the eyewitnesses make false charges, they may be flogged for perjury (24:4). ▶ See also **lian**.

Zionism the movement to create a homeland for **Jews** in the land of Israel. Zionism is the main cause of hostility between Jews and Muslims; before the rise of Zionism people of the two faiths lived harmoniously together in many societies.

Zuhd (*zooh-d*) asceticism; not setting one's heart on worldly things. It usually involves living extremely simply; not clinging to personal possessions such as **wealth**, or fine food and clothing; and perhaps practising various disciplines to strengthen spirituality, such as **fasting**, long sessions of **prayer** or study of the Qur'an and **dhikr**.

Zuhr or salat-ul-zuhr (*saa-lat-ul-zooh-r*) – the compulsory **salah** made just after the sun is at its height, but avoiding the actual moment of midday in case of association with sun-worship.

APPENDIX

The beautiful names of God

ad-Dar	The Distresser	al-Kabir	The Great
al-'Adl	The Just	al-Karim	The Magnanimous, the
al-'Afuw	The Forgiving		Generous, the Noble
al-Ahad	The One	al-Khabir	The Well-Informed
al-Akhir	The Last	al-Khatiq	The Creator
al-'Ali	The High One	al-Latif	The Gracious
al-'Alim	The Knowing	al-Majid	The Glorious
al-Awwal	The First	al-Malik	The King
al-'Azim	The Great	al-Matin	The Firm
al-'Aziz	The Mighty, and	al-Mubdi	The Founder
	also the Precious	al-Mudhill	The Abaser
al-Badl	The Originator	al-Mughni	The Enricher
al-Ba'ith	The Raiser	al-Muhaimin	The Vigilant, the
al-Baqi	The Enduring		Guardian
al-Bari	The Producer	al-Muhsi	The Counter
al-Barr	The Beneficent	al-Muhyi	The Giver of Life
al-Basir	The Seeing	al-Mu'id	The Restorer
al-Basit	The Expander	al-Mu'izz	The Honourer
al-Batin	The Inner	al-Mujib	The Responsive
al-Fattah	The Opener	al-Mu'min	The Giver of Peace
al-Ghaffar	The Forgiving	al-Mumit	The Slayer
al-Ghafur	The Pardoner	al-Muntaqim	The Avenger
al-Ghani	The Self-Sufficient	al-Muqaddim	The Bringer Forward
al-Hadi	The Guide	al-Muqit	The Maintainer, the
al-Hafiz	The Protector		Determiner, He Who
al-Hafiz	The Guardian		Brings to Pass
al-Hakam	The Judge	al-Muqsit	The Just
al-Hakim	The Wise	al-Muqtadir	The Prevailer
al-Halim	The Kindly	al-Murshid	The Guide
al-Hamid	The Praiseworthy	al-Musawwir	The Shaper
al-Haqq	The Truth	al-Muta'ali	The Self-Exalted
al-Hasib	The Accounter	al-Mutakabbir	The Superb
al-Hayy	The Living	al-Mu'ti	The Giver
al-Jabbar	The Irresistible	an-Nafi	The Propitious
al-Jami	The Gatherer	an-Nasir	The Helper

an-Nur	The Light	ar-Rahman	The Merciful
al-Qabid	The Seizer	ar-Raqib	The Vigilant
al-Qadir	The Capable	ar-Raqib	The Watchful
al-Qadir	The Powerful	ar-Ra'uf	The Gentle
al-Qahhar	The Victorious	ar-Razzaq	The Provider
al-Qahir	The Wise	as-Sabur	The Forbearing
al-Qawi	The Strong	as-Salam	The Peace
al-Qayyum	The Self-Subsistent	as-Samad	The Eternal
al-Quddus	The Holy	as-Sami	The Hearer
al-Wadud	The Loving	ash-Shahid	The Witness
al-Wahhab	The Bestower	ash-Shakur	The Appreciative
al-Wahid	The One	at-Tawwab	The Accepter of Repentance
al-Wakil	The Steward		
al-Wali	The Protector	at-Tawwab	The Relenting
al-Waliy	The Patron	az-Zahir	The Evident
al-Warith	The Inheritor	Dhu'l-Jalal wa'l-Ikram	The Lord of Majesty and Generosity
al-Wasi	The Vast		
ar-Rafi	The Exalter	Malik al-Mulk	Possessor of the Kingdom
ar-Rahim	The Compassionate		

The 25 prophets named in the Qur'an

Adam
Idris (Enoch)
Nuh (Noah)
Hud
Salih
Ibrahim (Abraham)
Isma'il (Ishmael)
Ishaq (Isaac)
Lut (Lot)
Yaqub (Jacob)
Yusuf (Joseph)
Shweib (Jethro)
Ayyub (Job)

Musa (Moses)
Harun (Aaron)
Dhulfikl (Ezekiel)
Dawud (David)
Suleiman (Solomon)
Ilias (Elijah)
Al-Yasa (Elisha)
Yunus (Jonah)
Zakariya (Zechariah)
Yahya (John the Baptist)
Isa (Jesus)
Muhammad

The adhan

Allahu Akbar (God is the Most Great)
(*four times*)

Ash-hadu an la ilaha il-allah (I bear
witness that there is no God but
Allah) (*twice*)

Ash-hadu ana Muhammad ar-
rasulullah (I bear witness that
Muhammad is the Prophet of
Allah) (*twice*)

Hayya alas salah (Come to prayer)
(*twice*)

Hayya alal falah (Come to success)
(*twice*)

Allahu Akbar (God is the Most Great)
(*twice*)

La ilaha il-allah (There is no God but
Allah) (*once*)

As-salutul khairum min an-naum (It
is better to pray than to sleep)
(*added in dawn prayer – once*)

The Fatihah

In the name of Allah, the
Compassionate, the Merciful.
All praise be to Allah,
The Lord of the worlds,
The Most Merciful, the Most Kind,
Master of the Day of Judgement.
You alone do we worship,
From You alone do we seek help.
Show us the next step
Along the straight path
Of those earning Your favour.
Keep us from the path of
Those earning Your anger,
Those who are going astray.

Muslim festivals

Month	Festivals	Duration
Muharram	• Muharram (New Year) • Ashurah (10th Muharram) – voluntary fast	1 day 2 days
Safar		
Rabi al-Awwal	• Maulid an-Nabi (12th Rabi al-Awwal)	1 day
Rabi al-Akhir		
Jumada al-Ula		
Jumada al-Akhrah		
Rajab	• Laylat-ul-Miraj (27th Rajab)	1 night
Shabaan	• Laylat-ul-Bara'at (14th Shabaan)	1 night
Ramadan	• Fasting • Laylat-ul-Qadr (27th Ramadan)	1 lunar month 1 night
Shawwal	• Id-ul-Fitr (1st Shawwal)	1 day
Dhul-Qidah		
Dhul-Hijjah	• Hajj • Id-ul-Adha (10th Dhul-Hijjah) • Sacrifice (11th and 12th Dhul-Hijjah)	5 days and nights 1 day 2 days

Map 1: The Muslim Empire by 732 CE

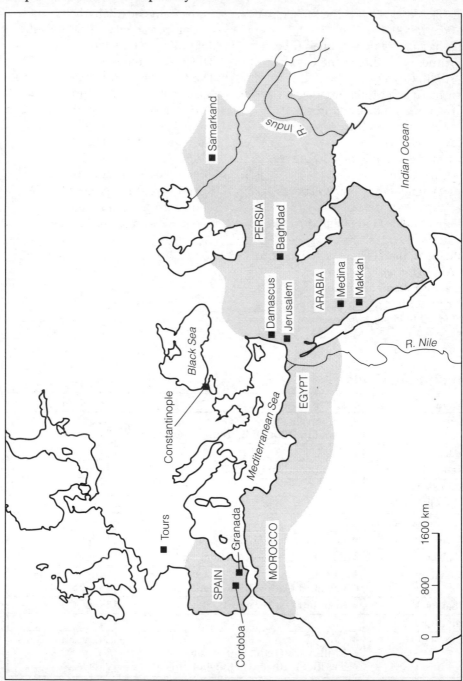

Map 2: The major Muslim dynasties in about 1600 CE

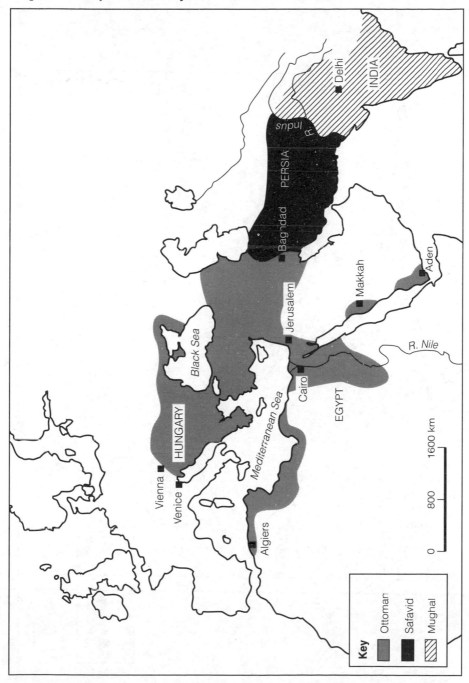

84

Map 3: The Muslim world today

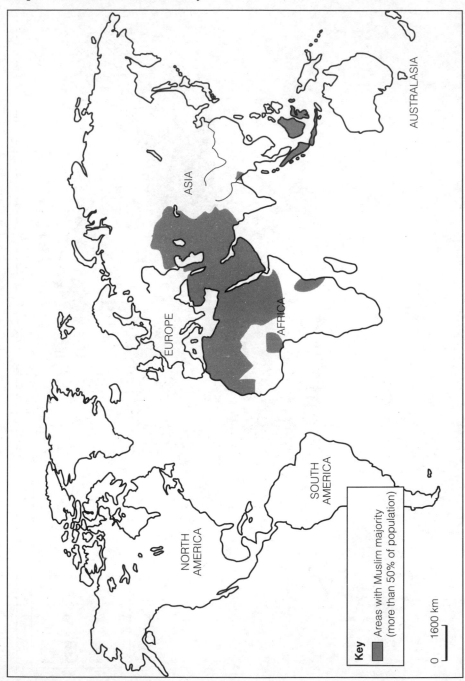

AUSTRALASIA

ASIA

EUROPE

AFRICA

SOUTH
AMERICA

NORTH
AMERICA

Key

Areas with Muslim majority
(more than 50% of population)

0   1600 km